Kopet: *A Documentary Narrative of Chief Joseph's Last Years*

KOPET

A Documentary Narrative

of Chief Joseph's Last Years

M. GIDLEY

UNIVERSITY OF WASHINGTON PRESS

Seattle and London

Copyright © 1981 by M. Gidley
Printed in the United States of America
Designed by Audrey Meyer

Library of Congress Cataloging in Publication Data

Gidley, M. (Mick)
    Kopet: a documentary narrative of Chief Joseph's
last years.

    Bibliography: p.
    Includes index.
    1. Joseph, Nez Percé Chief, 1840–1904.   2. Nez
Percé Indians—History.   3. Nez Percé Indians—
Biography.   I. Title.
E99.N5J5828   970.004′97 [B]   80–54428
ISBN 0–295–95794–8   AACR2

For Nancy—as ever

Contents

ILLUSTRATIONS

Cursed be the hand that scalps
the reputation of the dead.

—*saying attributed to Chief Joseph*

Preface

Chief Joseph and other Pacific Northwest Indian orators would often close formal speeches with the Chinook Jargon expression "kopet," a word which emphasizes the finality of what has been said and means something like "it is finished." *Kopet* seemed, therefore, a term appropriate for the title of a book on Joseph's own last years. I hope this book will not be thought of as a conventional biographical study of those years. It is not. It does not at all attempt, for example, to reconstruct or recreate what Joseph was thinking and feeling and it does not come near to describing his day-to-day life or many of the significant activities in which he played his part. Rather, it is highly selective and concerns those parts of his life that touched the lives of a number of white men at the turn of the century—and, of course those parts of *their* lives that touched his. The narrative is unfolded, therefore, largely through a series of documents, mainly letters and photographs produced by these men and newspaper items in which they figured. I believe that these men are interesting in their own right; one or two of them had remarkable careers—I am thinking especially of Edward S. Curtis, the photographer and writer—and the others offer us a direct insight into ordinary relationships between whites and Indians at the turn of the century. Then again, no relationship with Chief Joseph could have been ordinary because *he* was extraordinary.

Some inconsistencies of spelling and nomenclature will be apparent during the course of the book. The town now definitely known as Nespelem, for instance, was sometimes called Nespilem, and Peo-peo Tholekt's name occasioned an array of different spellings. I have attempted to be consistent in my own practice and have adopted those usages which seem most authoritative and clear. I have not tampered with anything in the quoted material, however, except to indicate omissions by ellipses and my own insertions by brackets. Thus, Dr. Latham's atrocious spelling and grammar are left as found, as is everyone's punctuation. This is a book which could easily have had masses of notes and an even lengthier bibliography than it has. In the interests of economy and fluency, I have chosen to indicate the sources of all the documents, including photographs, in the briefest form possible, at the conclusion of the narrative itself. The bibliographical essay is intended to point up certain materials rather than to offer an exhaustive list of items consulted.

I have reason to be grateful to many persons and institutions for help in bringing this book into existence; the following list is an admittedly inadequate acknowledgment of the fact. Richard Downar, Director of the American Studies Program, and the American Council of Learned Societies awarded me an American Studies Fellowship for 1976–77. The University of Exeter granted me leave and financial assistance. The British Academy and the American Philosophical Society gave me grants towards research in the United States in the summer of 1978. George Quimby, Director, and the staff of the Thomas Burke Memorial Washington State Museum at the University of Washington, provided hospitality and encouragement during my research in Seattle.

The following provided materials for publication in this book and, often, much additional assistance: Gary Lundell and the Records Center of the University of Washington Libraries; Robert D. Monroe, Head, and Dennis Andersen of the Photography Collection of the University of Washington's Suzzallo Library; Andrew Johnson, Head, Glenda Pearson and other staff of the Northwest Collection at the Suzzallo Library; David Piff and the Federal Archives and Records Center, Seattle; Terry Abraham of the Manuscript, Archives, and Special Collections Division of the Washington State University Library, Pullman; the History Section of Seattle Public Library; Barbara Townsend and the Montana Historical Society, Helena; Ken Duckett, Phil Zorich, the late Martin Schmitt, and the Oregon Collection of the University of Oregon, Eugene; Ellen Welsh and other staff of the Maryhill Museum, Goldendale; James Glenn and other staff of the National Anthropological Archives, Washington, D.C.; the Oregon Historical Society, Portland; W. S. Phillips; Leonard Eshom, Ellis Jones, and the Rainier Club, Seattle; Robert Ruby; and the University of Exeter Library.

The following individuals and staffs gave me significant information, often by mail and sometimes by granting access to materials: Nadene Miller and the Reference Section of Spokane Public Library; Richard Berner, Head, and the Manuscripts Collection, University of Washington Libraries; the Art Division, Seattle Public Library; the staff of the Library of Eastern Washington State Historical Society, Spokane; Frank Greene and the Library of the Washington State Historical Society, Tacoma; Richard Crawford of the National Resources Division of the National Archives, Washington, D.C.; Nita Becker and the Jerome Public Library, Idaho; Mary Winter and the Kentucky Historical Society Library, Frankfort; George Frykman; Charles Issetts, Head, the History of the Health Sciences Library, University of Cincinnati Medical Center; Terrence Kaufman; Michael Silverstein; Jay Miller; and Lewis Saum.

James Nason and Merle Wells gave me valuable advice on the structure of the book. By typing and offering secretarial assistance, Angela Day, Susan Harshberger, and Sandra Skinner have helped me to complete it. Sean Goddard produced the map.

None of the above should be thought responsible for errors of fact or judgment; I hope that any that there are will be seen as matters of omission rather than commission, for I attempted to follow the advice implied in the saying attributed to Chief Joseph that is used here as an epigraph. The dedication to my wife is, of course, inadequate.

M.G.

I. Starting Out
from the Meany Papers

AN INTRODUCTION

T HIS book was derived, so to speak, by opportunism out of serendipity. For another purpose altogether—a projected biographical and critical study of Edward S. Curtis, author, anthropologist, and photographer— I was reading Curtis' letters to Edmond S. Meany. These form a small and interspersed component of Professor Meany's papers stored in the Records Center of the institution Meany did so much to build and at which he taught for four decades, the University of Washington in Seattle. Meany was endowed with enormous energies. He had barely attained manhood when his father, a tugboat captain, was drowned in the Skagit River north of Seattle, and from then on he had to shoulder the responsibilities of family care. The capacity for hard work that he brought to his various jobs—from newspaper boy to reporter, legislator, and teacher—was also apparent in his correspondence. It was extensive; often he would write ten or twenty letters in the course of a morning, and he seems to have kept almost everything. As Meany was friendly with Curtis for more than a quarter of a century, the Curtis letters now appear in many of the collection's chronologically arranged folders. While I rummaged through these folders my eye was naturally looking out for references to Curtis and, because Curtis worked with over eighty different Native American peoples, to Indians in general. I read any letter on U.S. Indian Service paper.

So it came to pass that, over a number of days, with many other letters intervening, I took in, and was absorbed by, the correspondence with Meany of Henry M. Steele, Edward H. Latham, and Barnett Stillwell, all resident for several years at Nespelem on the Colville Reservation in eastern Washington, the place where Chief Joseph's band of Nez Perces were quartered during Joseph's last years (and where many of the band's descendants still remain). Each of these men knew Joseph well, or, at least, was in a position to do so. Steele was the Bureau of Indian Affairs farmer employed to try to teach the Nez Perces how to farm well enough to support themselves; later he became a notary public at Nespelem. Latham was an Indian agency physician who was based at Nespelem for most of his long service. Stillwell ran the Indian day school at Nespelem for several years.

The Records Center where I worked has no windows; stacks of boxes and files reach to the ceiling in rows throughout the building, cutting off any expansive view of the interior; except for the whirring of a fan heater high on a metal wall behind me, there were no appreciable noises. The archivists there wear white overall coats rather like those of laboratory technicians and tend to move silently as they lift folders, boxes, and ledgers in and out of place. While I have sometimes felt claustrophobic in the Records Center, it is a place without distractions. These factors may have contributed somewhat to the sense of shock I felt when I read Dr. Latham's account of Henry Steele's end—although anyone who has had the temerity to read the relevant part of this book before scanning these introductory remarks will probably understand the degree of my surprise. Steele's letters had revealed a man who, having married and become a father at a relatively advanced age, openly delighted in the life of his immediate family, especially the foibles of his young daughter, Irene. He also, it seemed to me, possessed a capacious and sympathetic awareness of his fellow men in general, perhaps more such awareness than was displayed by almost all of the other people whose letters I was reading. Yet he came home one day and slit his daughter's throat, nearly severing her head from her body, and then killed himself. I felt compelled to go back through the folders for some explanation of what he had done: not one of them contained any intimation of the horror to come. With that failure, I started to look elsewhere. First I searched the records of the Colville Reservation, which are now kept at the Federal Archives and Records Center in Seattle, and then the papers of a man Steele respected, who was ultimately responsible for Colville Reservation affairs at the time of these deaths, Agent John McA. Webster. The latter are in the library of Washington State University at Pullman. I pursued the remarks of relevant newspaper accounts, especially those easier to catch as they lay within the borders of the obituary columns. Some results of my searches are reproduced in full or in part in this book.

I also looked for photographs associated with the various men mentioned, and here—though I found no certain likeness of Henry Steele and only poor ones of Edward Latham and Barnett Stillwell—I feel rewarded. Meany was a keen amateur photographer who took his camera with him when he made his first visit to Nespelem in 1901, and, more important for our purposes, he collected photographs as historical documents. This accounts for the survival of many of the pictures reproduced here, for they were part of Meany's bequest to the University of Washington. Edward S. Curtis was a major professional photographic artist, and I feel privileged to be able to present in this book some of his work that has not been previously published, as well as a couple of his justifiably famous images of Chief Joseph. Dr. Latham—as my own recent study based on his images, *With One Sky Above Us* (1979), testifies—was an amateur photographer of considerable ability. Many of his photographs reproduced in this book have not appeared before, and I hope that they will further alert those interested in the history of photography to the true scope and quality of his achievement. Whether produced with conscious skill by known photographers like Lee Moorhouse of Pendleton, Oregon, or snapped one sunny afternoon by an anonymous enthusiast, the other images here are also not mere embellishments but are integral to the record, bear witness, and constitute, so to speak, additional testimony.

But they have nothing to say about Steele's final acts. For those there is, of course, no satisfactory explanation, in light on emulsion, in ink, in print, or anywhere else. It is likely, as indeed Steele's brother thought, that his last destructive deeds were intimately related, in some perverse manner, to the very sensitivity and moral awareness I had noticed in his letters. But it seemed increasingly absurd to contemplate the profoundest motivations of a figure so shadowy, and my gaze widened, almost involuntarily, to try to encompass some of the other links already hinted at: Meany and Curtis; Meany and Steele,

Latham, Stillwell, and Webster; these Colville Reservation residents with each other; and all of them with the Indians. When I reread the letters to Meany of Steele, Curtis, Latham, and Stillwell, as well as those of two sharply contrasting Indian agents, John McA. Webster and his predecessor, Albert M. Anderson—all of them, like Meany, immigrants to the present Northwest from the Old Northwest—they seemed to form themselves into a kind of pattern, and not one that Meany, their original recipient, could have apprehended when he received them more than a biblical lifetime ago.

Meany, as we shall see, had hopes for a time of writing a full-scale biography of Chief Joseph. He collected material for it of all kinds, and I was fortunate enough to stumble upon much of this in his papers, along with certain rare items that emanated from the Chief himself. A couple of Chief Joseph's letters to Meany and transcriptions of speeches he delivered on occasions that Meany organized are published here for the first time. On balance though, I do not believe that the new primary material adds substantially to the sum total of available *information* on Joseph. It is true that most existing biographical and historical studies end with his eloquent speech of surrender amidst the driving snow of the Nez Perce War's last battle in 1877, with only a cursory glance at his remaining twenty-five years of life; but Joseph in exile at Nespelem lived in proximity to Chief Moses of the Columbias, so anyone especially interested in Joseph's later career could have deduced much from the full account of Moses' life provided by Robert H. Ruby and John A. Brown in *Half-Sun on the Columbia* (1965). The present book offers rather more in the way of *interpretation* than information, a rounding out of the received version of Joseph's figure so that he appears more human—if, of necessity, more vulnerable, sometimes stubborn, perhaps even petty at times. Indeed, his mythical status is brought into question somewhat; but more on this later.

The book has a double focus: not Chief Joseph alone, but also some of the whites who knew him in his last years and with whom both he and Meany were in contact. I think of them as witnesses to Joseph's end and also as protagonists in their own right. The story of their interaction with Joseph and with each other (both all too hazily perceived, I am sure) may not add substantially to the known portrait of the last great chief of the Nez Perce people, but it should help to realign the critical frame in which it resides. Sketches of these men follow.

ALBERT M. ANDERSON (1862–1928), businessman and U.S. Indian agent. Born and orphaned in Wisconsin, Anderson arrived in Spokane Falls, eastern Washington, in 1877. He attended school for a couple of years, then clerked and kept store for a number of men, first at Fort Colville, then at Fort Spokane near the Colville Reservation. He was appointed clerk and chief assistant to the agent for the Colville Reservation in 1889. He remained in this position until 1893 when he went to Olympia, Washington, the state capital, first as a clerk in the office of Secretary of State J. H. Price and then in the Bureau of

Statistics. It was while working in Olympia that he first met Edmond S. Meany.

He was appointed agent to the Colville Reservation and took the title of major in 1897. While Anderson was enthusiastic about the opening of the "North Half" of the vast reservation to white settlement, his annual reports to the Commissioner for Indian Affairs spoke strongly against the encroachment of individual prospectors and larger mining interests onto the "South Half," which was not thrown open until after what was known as the McLaughlin Agreement of 1910. In 1902 he was sued personally for resisting these incursions into Indian lands, but was vindicated in the courts. Nevertheless, in 1903, the year of his marriage to Ella Reuner and a year before Chief Joseph's death, he was summarily removed from his post after an investigation of gross irregularities in the agency accounts. He entered the real estate business, which—with the rapid growth of his adopted village Spokane Falls into the city of Spokane—was very profitable; he came to own large and valuable properties. In 1906 he became right-of-way and tax agent for the Great Northern Railway, in which capacity he bought development land for the railroad, including land supposedly held in perpetuity by the Indians of the Colville and Spokane reservations. He remained right-of-way agent for the railroad until his death, and was apparently greatly esteemed by its president, Ralph Budd.

EDWARD S. CURTIS (1868–1952). Curtis was born in Wisconsin and grew to early manhood there and in Minnesota. In 1887 he migrated to Sidney, now known as Port Orchard, across Puget Sound from Seattle. By 1892 Curtis was a partner in a Seattle photographic studio and later—though he was always assisted by family members, particularly his nephew by marriage, William W. Phillips, and by professional operatives, notably Adolf F. Muhr—he came into sole charge of one that established itself as, perhaps, the leading portrait studio in the city.

In about 1895 Curtis started to photograph local Indians, making mainly portraits and genre studies, which won prizes in major photographic competitions. By the turn of the century his Indian collection had achieved fame throughout the Northwest. Curtis was also a leading member of the Portland-based mountaineering club, the Mazamas, through which he met several national figures in the natural history field. In a few short years, through a fusion of artistic ability, ambition, hard work, and friendship with men of influence, he made pictures among a dozen widely dispersed Indian peoples, served on the executive committee and as official photographer of the Harriman Alaska Expedition of 1899, lectured at such institutions as the National Geographic Society and the Century Club, wrote for *Scribner's*, photographed President Theodore Roosevelt and his family, and exhibited at the Cosmos Club in Washington, D.C., and the Waldorf-Astoria in New York City.

From about 1900, Curtis began to conceive of building his Indian work into a comprehensive pictorial record of a people he thought of as a "vanishing race." He used his studio profits to fund the work, and vainly approached possible patrons, including the Smithsonian's Bureau of American Ethnology. He and his assistants also started to collect a written record of the various tribes visited. He met Chief Joseph in 1903 and collected data among the Nez Perces in 1905 and during various summers for a number of years. Early in 1906 J. Pierpont Morgan was persuaded to subsidize the fieldwork involved in the production of what was to prove Curtis' major work, *The North American Indian* (1907–30). This was eventually printed in twenty volumes of illustrated text and twenty portfolios of photogravures in a severely limited edition. Curtis thought, initially, that the task would take about fifteen years; he threw his whole weight into it and also took on the job of securing subscriptions to the publication. In an ultimate sense the work, which took nearly thirty years to complete, is an outstanding monument to what is probably the largest anthropological project ever undertaken by one man and a group of assistants. Moreover, though others helped with the gathering of data and William E. Myers was increasingly responsible for the bulk of the text, Curtis did take all the photographs and these, we now realize, constitute a major work of art. The venture was exciting but also exacting. Curtis worked at it compulsively and obsessively, and it helped to break his marriage and harm his health. After finishing it he turned his hand to other things, including gold mining, but nothing could ever match the stimulation of those first years of "the work," as he usually called it. Even before the completion of *The North American Indian*, his fame had lessened, and his photography declined into virtual oblivion until the revival early in the 1970s.

EDWARD H. LATHAM (1845–1928), physician and photographer. Latham was born in Columbus, Ohio. Almost nothing is known of his early life. In 1870 he married Mary Archer of New Richmond, Ohio. In the following fifteen years they had three sons and both Lathams received medical degrees from teaching institutions in Cincinnati, Ohio. The couple set up a joint practice, first in Cincinnati, then briefly in Kentucky, but in 1887 they sought the more salubrious climate of Spokane and established themselves there. While Edward quietly practiced his profession and busied himself with his hobby, photography, Mary Latham rapidly became the most prominent woman doctor in the Northwest, especially as she was also involved in various community activities, including the founding of Spokane's public library.

In 1890 Latham was appointed agency physician on the Colville Reservation with a single man's quarters at Nespelem, over a hundred miles by wagon road from Spokane. He and his wife drifted apart, were divorced in 1900, and she died in 1917. The *Annual Report of the Commissioner of Indian Affairs* for 1889 speaks of the life of a physician on an Indian reservation "with poor accommodations, small salary, and few of the modern appliances and help" as "dreary enough to all except to him who realizes the noble part he may perform in helping to lift this people out of their superstitious regard for the grotesque need of the 'medicine men'."[1]

Latham seems to have taken such views seriously, at least during his early years on the reservation. In his report for the *Annual Report* of 1892 he outlined without complaint the enormous size of his practice and the lack of a hospital and proper medical supplies, and he characterized the various tribes within his jurisdiction according to their reverence for western medical notions. During the winter of 1900 he had to contend with a serious outbreak of smallpox, especially among the Nez Perce people, and there were rumors that he did not give the quarantined Indians the care they needed. Again, in 1908, there were similar complaints and Agent Webster, in his efficiency report on agency staff for 1909, wrote of Latham: "Is a superannuated gentleman who has not kept up with his profession, and has vegetated and hibernated at Nespelem for the past 18 years; is kindly, hospitable and charitable; has accumulated enough money to buy a nice place on Lake Chelan, which has increased in value since he purchased it. He has exhibited more energy in the past year, but is too old and indolent to be efficient, and I rate him 'Fair'."[2] Whatever his medical record, Latham claimed to have been befriended by several influential Indians, especially Chief Moses of the Columbias who died in 1899, but also by Joseph himself and Chica-ma-poo, the oldest survivor among Joseph's band at Nespelem, a woman who is said to have fought like a man during the Nez Perce War of 1877. In 1910 Latham retired to his house on Lake Chelan where he lived quietly until his death.

EDMOND S. MEANY (1862–1935), educator and historian. Born in East Saginaw, Michigan, Meany was brought west by his family. He was tall, redheaded, vain, gregarious, and remarkably energetic. More than is the case with most public figures, his personal life and his public activities were inextricably bonded together, a seamless web. In 1889 Meany married Sarah Elizabeth Ward and by her had four children, two of whom survived him; even this most private of relationships had its professional aspect: he met her while collecting historical data from her pioneer father. He was indelibly associated with the University of Washington for half a century as a student, legislator, administrator, and teacher; indeed, he himself was a tradition. It seems most fitting, therefore, to communicate his brief biography in the form of an academic curriculum vitae:

Degrees

1885	B.S.	University of Washington
1899	M.S.	University of Washington
1901	M.Litt	University of Wisconsin
1926	LLD.(Hon.)	College of Puget Sound

Appointments and Honors

1880–84	Various small business activities in Seattle
1885–90	Cub-reporter; then City Editor and Night Editor, *Seattle Post-Intelligencer*
1891–94	Member, House of Representatives, State of Washington, and Secre-

tary, State of Washington Commission, World's Columbian Exposition, Chicago, 1893

1894–97	Secretary, Board of Regents, University of Washington
1895–97	Registrar and Lecturer on Northwest History and Forestry, University of Washington
1897–1935	Professor of History and Chairman, History Department, University of Washington
1906–09	Secretary, Commission, Alaska-Yukon-Pacific Exposition, Seattle, 1909
1909–35	President, Mountaineers, Seattle
1913–14	President, Pacific Coast branch, American Historical Association
1921–35	Executive Commissioner, Seattle area, Boy Scouts of America
1926–27	Vice President, Pacific Coast branch, American Alpine Club
1929	Chevalier, Legion of Honor

Editorial Activities

1888–89	Co-editor, *Seattle Daily Trade Journal* and *Puget Sound Magazine*
1899–1901	Editor, Christmas editions, *Argus*, Seattle
1900	Editor, *Alaska Magazine*
1906	Editor, *Washington Magazine*
1906–35	Executive editor, *Washington Historical Quarterly*

Selected Publications

Books

1900	Ed., *Art Work of the State of Washington* (Oshkosh, Wis.: Art Photographs Co.)
1907	Ed., *Vancouver's Discovery of Puget Sound* (New York: Macmillan)
1909	*History of the State of Washington* (New York: Macmillan, rev. ed., 1924)
1911	*Mountain Camp Fires* (verse) (Seattle: Lowman and Hanford)
1912	*United States History for Schools* (New York: Macmillan)
1916	Ed., *Mount Rainier, A Record of Exploration* (New York: Macmillan)
1927	*The Pacific Northwest, A Syllabus* (Seattle: L. G. Wilkins)
1931	*Washington from Life* (Seattle: Frank McCaffrey)
1933	*Lincoln Esteemed Washington* (Seattle: Frank McCaffrey)

Articles

1889	"Has Puget Sound a Literature?" *Washington Magazine* 1 (September):8–11
1903	"Attu and Yakutat Basketry," *Pacific Monthly* 10 (October):211–19
1904	"Fox Farming in Alaska," *Out West* 21 (August):114–30
1906	"Alaskan Mummies," *Washington Magazine* 1 (August):459–68
1907	"Last Survivor of the Oregon Mission of 1840," *Washington Historical Quarterly* 2 (October):12–23
1908	"Hunting Indians with a Camera," *World's Work* 15 (March): 10,004–11
1909	"[The Foreloper, a Lost Kipling Poem]," *Century Magazine* 77 (January):471–72; widely reprinted, with Kipling's poem
1911	"The Olympic National Monument," *The Mountaineer* 4:54–59

| 1914 | "A New Lincoln Portrait Discovered," *Harper's Weekly* 58 (14 February):10–11 |
| 1916 | "First American Settlement on Puget Sound," *Washington Historical Quarterly* 7 (April):136–43 |

Newspaper articles

1901	"Historical Geography," a series of six articles in the *Seattle Times* from 2 February to 20 March
1905	"Survey of the Native Races of Washington," a series of twenty-five articles in the *Seattle Post-Intelligencer* from 18 June to 12 November
1911	"Random Remiscences of Thirty-three Years at the University of Washington," a series in the University of Washington's *Washingtonian* for April, May, and June
1915	"Governors of Washington," a series in the *Seattle Post-Intelligencer* from 27 September to 22 October
1915–16	"Living Pioneers of Washington," a series of 195 biographical articles in the *Seattle Post-Intelligencer* from 27 October 1915 to 3 June 1916

HENRY M. STEELE (1863–1908), pioneer. Born in DePere (Brown County), Wisconsin, of Canadian and Irish parents, Steele graduated from high school there and then taught school before migrating westwards with his elder brother, George. The brothers farmed in Montana for a time before taking jobs under the Bureau of Indian Affairs on the Colville Reservation in 1893. George was employed as a carpenter for a number of years and eventually set up his own business in Coeur d'Alene, Idaho. Henry was appointed as an additional farmer or farmer, whose task, as defined by the Bureau of Indian Affairs, was not only to give a lead in practical farming by modern methods, but also to encourage and teach Indians to farm profitably.

The *Annual Report of the Commissioners of Indian Affairs* for 1889, asks each agent to consider, among other things, whether his farmer is "a man of good moral character, strictly temperate, and disposed to treat the Indians kindly, and with patience and consideration for their peculiarities, so that he has secured their confidence and respect."[3] Steele was based at Nespelem, sixty miles from agency headquarters at Miles. He was a subagent assigned to work primarily with Chief Joseph's band. As the Colville reservation was huge, he performed the functions of an agent himself as far as the Indians in the vicinity of Nespelem were concerned. He quickly learned the Chinook Jargon used by many Northwest Indians for communication with other tribes and with whites, and also the Nez Perce language. When Erskine Wood, son of C. E. S. Wood (General O. O. Howard's aide during the 1877 Nez Perce War), came to stay in Joseph's home on the reservation for the second time, in 1893, Steele acted as occasional companion to the fourteen-year-old white boy and gave him odd jobs, such as helping distribute rations.

Steele knew the territory and its people as well as any white man of his time. He was allocated the job of enumerating the population of the reservation for the 1900 census and the enormity of the task may be surmised from the following letter sent by Agent Anderson to Austin Mires, census director:

. . . such a vast territory cannot be properly enumerated within the prescribed time. A very conservative estimate of the population in that district (whites and Indians) is from 1,800 to 2,000, and considering the expanse of territory to cover to get this number of people it will require more than thirty days. The white people are scattered throughout the mountains and sometimes it is necessary to travel from 10 to 20 miles to get 4 or 5 names. Every tributary to the San Poil River has prospectors and the trails are almost inaccessible.[4]

Just before his death Steele made, from horseback travel, what was judged to be an accurate map of the "South Half." In August 1900, for a variety of reasons, Steele resigned from the Indian service, although he did not leave Nespelem and remained close to his Nez Perce friends. He worked for a local merchant, recorded the gold findings of the increasing numbers of whites with mines on the reservation, and became a notary. During his first years in Nespelem he boarded at a house rented from the Indian service by Rosemary Alice Shaffer, whose family farmed in Douglas County across the Columbia River. Miss Shaffer, born in Iowa and five years younger than Steele, was one of the very few unmarried white women in a vast sparsely populated land, and she was the only unmarried white woman in Nespelem. In September 1903 she and Steele were married and a year or so later their child, Irene, was born. The Shaffer boarding house became Steele's Hotel run by 'Mary Steele, and Henry had his office there. After Henry's death—what old-time Nespelem resident Lora Beggs, in a pamphlet titled *Nespelem—Then and Now*, called "our first tragedy"—Mrs. Steele sold the hotel to Sam Iames. In about 1915, however, she returned to Nespelem, built a new fourteen-room hotel to replace the original log structure, and ran it for a number of years. This place, even after her departure, was known as Steele's Hotel until it burned down sometime in the twenties.

BARNETT STILLWELL (1864–1928), businessman and teacher. Born in Wisconsin, Stillwell and his wife Dema, to whom he was married in 1888, had both traveled about the West a good deal before settling down in 1897, as teacher and housekeeper, respectively, at the new Nespelem Day School on the Colville Reservation. At first both Chief Joseph and Chief Moses had vigorously opposed sending the children of their two tribes to the school, but Stillwell seems to have won them over in time. His two daughters, Ada born in 1889 and Emma born a year later, learned the Chinook Jargon and, possibly, the Nez Perce tongue; Ada frequently interpreted for Joseph and other Nez Perces during transactions with whites.

On the closure of the Nespelem Day School in 1901 (it was reopened some years later but Stillwell declined to apply for the job of teacher), Stillwell and his family moved to Chelan. The teacher became a real estate man, first in partnership with Robert A. Steaves, then on his own. Operating under the slogan "the time to sell is when the other fellow wants to buy, the time to buy is when the other fellow wants to sell," Stillwell built up a fair business before moving to Jerome, Idaho, in about 1910. In Jerome, while remaining in real estate, he also gave rein to some of his political instincts and at various times held posts in the town's government, including justice of the peace and treasurer.

JOHN MCADAM WEBSTER (1849–1921), U.S. army officer and Indian agent. Webster was born in Warrenton, Ohio, and reared in Steubenville, Ohio. His father was killed in the Union invasion of Kentucky in 1862. He served in the 197th Ohio Volunteer Infantry from April to July 1865; commissioned second lieutenant at age sixteen. He then joined the regular army: cadet, U.S. Military Academy, West Point, 1865–1871; commissioned second lieutenant, 22nd Infantry Regiment, 1871; frontier service thereafter in a number of western states; married Rose S. Van Allen at Fort MacKenzie, Minnesota, 1874; promoted to first lieutenant, 1879, and to captain, 1891; accidental severe injury damaged use of right leg, making a stick mandatory, 1895; retired from military service to private life in Steubenville, 1898.

On the recommendation (unsolicited) of the Commander of the Army, he was appointed by the Bureau of Indian Affairs as superintendent of the Colville Agency in 1904. He met Chief Joseph, who died the same year. He tried to protect the Indians in his charge from the encroachments of railroads, mining companies, and settlers seeking land, and proved tireless in this losing battle. His own attitudes towards Indians were expressed in a Seattle speech, "Preparing the Indians for Self Support and Citizenship," which he delivered in 1909. He was party to the McLaughlin Agreement, which opened up the "South Half" of the Colville Reservation to white settlement. In 1912 he resigned, but was persuaded to return to eastern Washington in 1913 as superintendent of the Spokane Reservation. He resigned for the last time in 1914 and died in retirement at Mackinaw Island, Michigan, in 1921.

While obviously not a cross-section of Pacific Northwest society at the turn of the century, these seven figures do represent a varied range of professions and pursuits. At the same time, they do seem, in retrospect, to have had things in common other than that they all knew Chief Joseph. They were male, all immigrants to the Pacific Northwest who, in turn, had been born into pioneer families in the Middle West. They were not all successful in the usual worldly meaning of the term, but each had something of an eye for the main chance; even Steele, who was relatively unambitious, believed, as we shall see, that he was materially bettering himself when he left the Indian service. Also, with the exceptions of Curtis and Meany, each of these men knew Chief Joseph as a result of being employed by the Bureau of Indian Affairs and being responsible for at least aspects of life on the Colville Reservation.

Finally, a psychological speculation may be in order. It is a curious fact that, with the possible exception of Stillwell, each man had lost his father before attaining manhood: when Latham was only three years old, his father died;

and the other fathers died when their sons were still teenagers. It may be that Joseph—who was both chief and father to his people, and who had no son to succeed him—assumed a special position in the psyches of these orphaned men that cannot now be openly discerned but which helped to determine their sympathetic or hostile responses to him.

A great deal is known about the activities of the Nez Perce people through most of the period of regular contact with whites, and Joseph's actions (together with those of other Nez Perce leaders) have been narrated in impressive detail, especially by Alvin Josephy in *The Nez Perce Indians and the Opening of the Northwest* (1965). The Chronology in this book gives but a brief and bare recital of the record. Paradoxically, on the reservation years there is much less information available. In the course of the following few paragraphs I will try to provide an outline of the history and workings of the Colville Reservation around the turn of the century.

The Colville Reservation, home to about two thousand Indians during Joseph's last years, was established in 1872. It was bounded by the Canadian border to the north, the Okanogan River to the west, and a great bend of the Columbia River to the south and east. This is a vast territory of forest and arid uplands with several dominating rivers and divisive, if small, mountain ranges, so that it is not surprising that it was inhabited by a number of distinctly different Salish-speaking peoples: the Nespelems in the Nespelem Valley, the San Poils along the banks of the San Poil River, and the Lakes in the northeast section. The traditional territories of the Colvilles on the eastern edge and the Okanogans on the western edge were divided by the reservation boundary. In addition, the Spokanes and the Columbias often visited the territory and hunted over it. The Spokanes were eventually allocated a reservation of their own to the southeast of the Colville Reservation, though the same agent served both. The Columbias, Chief Moses' people, had formerly roamed all over the middle Columbia region and at one point were offered a reservation of their own to the west of the Colville, but they were ultimately allocated to the Colville and most of them settled in the Nespelem Valley.

The settlement of the Columbias in the Nespelem Valley was resented by the Nespelems and the San Poils. Their opposition was expressed most forcefully by the severely crippled messianic leader of the San Poils, Skolaskin. While Moses and his people were prepared to take government rations, Skolaskin and his followers refused any aid, partly because they wished to keep to themselves and their own traditions, and partly because they would not accept anything that might be construed as payment for lands they had not intended to forfeit and which they still considered their own. These frictions were greatly exacerbated when, in 1885, largely through the influence of Moses, Chief Joseph's band of Nez Perces were also brought to the Nespelem Valley where already some five hundred Indians were living.

The Nez Perces shared the same Plateau culture as the Salish-speaking tribes, but, like the Yakimas and the Cayuses, they were members of the Shahaptian

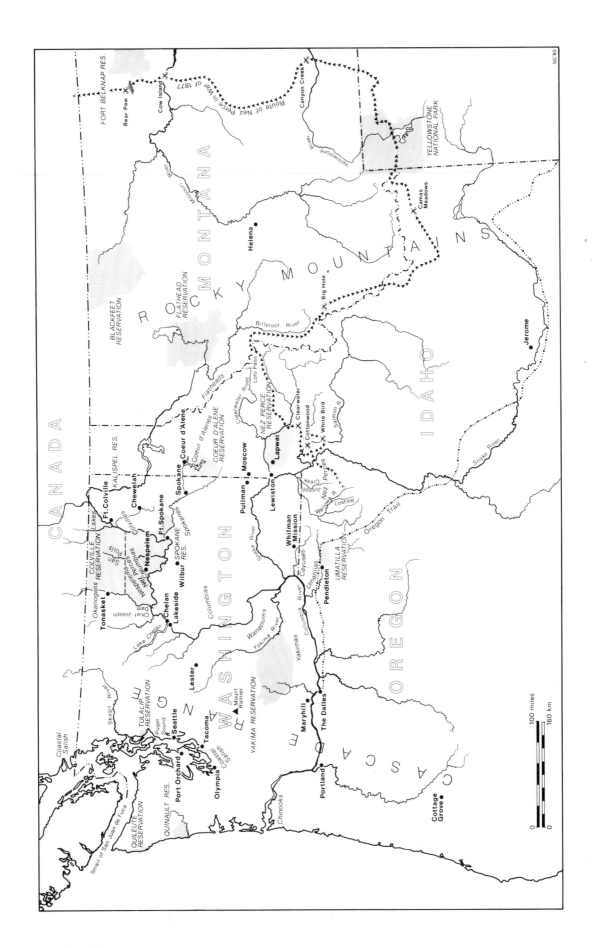

language-family and had never resided in the territory covered by the Colville Reservation. They were, in effect, exiles. At their defeat in the 1877 Nez Perce War they were transported to Indian Territory on the southern plains and, as the Chronology section here records, they were not allowed to return to the Northwest until 1885. Then, for nearly a year, they were relegated to an insanitary camp adjacent to the agency headquarters at Chewelah. Some, including the followers of Chief Yellow Bull, elected to stay there, but, with the fall advancing, most of them proceeded to Nespelem. Skolaskin immediately led a large band of Salish to oppose their settlement. For several hours there was much tension and the threat of bloodshed. The agent, Major Rickard K. Gwydir, had to call in a detachment of troops to restore calm.

The Nez Perces were also aliens and exceptions on the reservation in other respects. Joseph and most of the Nez Perces deposited on the Colville were from the Wallowa Valley in northeastern Oregon. They had never given up their claim to their original homeland and for many years after their arrival in the Nespelem Valley they cherished a desire to return there. In the case of Joseph himself the wish to return to the land of his birth remained the guiding principle behind many of his public pronouncements until his death in 1904.

When the Nez Perces who survived the harsh years in Indian Territory were returned to the Northwest, most of those who professed to be Christians were placed on the Nez Perce Reservation in Idaho. Most of Joseph's followers were not Christians. They were Dreamers. Dreamers were followers of the teachings of the Wanapum leader Smohalla. Smohalla reaffirmed traditional Indian values of total reverence for the earth. In practice, although the cult was against white incursions into Indian culture, it was strongly influenced by evangelical Christianity and ceremonies often involved testimony by one or more of the participants as well as drumming and bells. In their reverence for the earth the Dreamers refused to countenance the parceling up of land and, even more vehemently, the tilling of the soil. "You ask me to plough the ground," said Smohalla. "Shall I take a knife and tear my mother's breast? Then when I die she will not take me to her bosom to rest."[5]

Adherence to the Dreamer religion meant that most of the Nez Perces could readily graze horses as they had always done with much success, but they would not learn to plant corn and potatoes. As there was a declining market and use for their pony herds, they found themselves at odds with the new economic order. Also, when they were forced to capitulate, possibly by picking hops in the Yakima Valley as seasonal laborers, their sense of humiliation was intense. Normally, they were heavily dependent on government beef rations for food and frequently went hungry. In their efforts to keep to the habits and tenets of their own culture they were brought up sharply against the dictates of the reservation authorities. The following extracts from Major Anderson's reports in the *Annual Report of the Commissioner for Indian Affairs* are typical:

I venture to state, without fear of contradiction, that no tribe under the jurisdiction of this agency has received the attention and assistance from the Government that Chief Joseph and his band have. Regardless of this, . . . they have been persistent in following their ancient traditions and indulging in their primitive customs. . . . They are strictly "blanket" Indians, and their dress on frequent occasions is hideous in appearance and possesses many of the characteristics of the Indian in his native state. They have no religion, believe in no creed, and their morality is at a low ebb. . . . Closer restrictions should be thrown around them, and by abolishing the issue of subsistence and clothing to them they will be on an equal footing with other progressive tribes in the same locality.[6] *[1898]*

On [their] small farms the Government has erected comfortable and suitable houses for their occupancy, but none of them is ever occupied. Chief Joseph himself does not occupy the house erected on his farm, and has not resided on his farm to my certain knowledge for the past seven years. He, with his handful of unworthy followers, prefers the traditional tepee, living on the generosity of the Government and passing away their time in a filthy and licentious way of living. . . . History has been partial to Joseph in chronicling his atrocious acts. . . . The appalling wrongs done by him are crying from the bloodstained soil of Idaho for restitution.[7] *[1900]*

The extreme hostility evident in Anderson's views was, of course, not shared by all Bureau employees, but the objectives of his policy were. And the Nez Perces, as the second quotation indicates, were considered prisoners undergoing punishment for their part in the 1877 war. Consequently, their movements were curtailed and, at times, they were spied upon.

The fact that so many Nez Perces, including some from Joseph's band, were settled two hundred miles from Nespelem on the Nez Perce Reservation in Idaho, meant that individual Nez Perces were always trying to visit relatives and friends. This led not only to trouble with the agency authorities but also to a degree of instability in the Nespelem Nez Perce community. At the same time, when Joseph called gatherings of the Nez Perces for Fourth of July and other celebrations, the Nez Perces were sustained in their own traditions by the assembled kinspeople from Idaho and further afield. In their alien new home they would race their horses as of old, gamble, dance, conduct traditional ceremonies, and, in general, reaffirm their identities as members of a proud nation.

The Nespelem Nez Perces may also be viewed as exceptions to the rule on the Colville Reservation in that they fared exceptionally badly under the terms of the Allotment Act of 1887. The whole thrust of Bureau of Indian Affairs policy in the last two decades of the nineteenth century and the first two of the twentieth century was to break down Native American cultures and to make Indians over into surrogate whites who would enter the mainstream of American life, though without, of course, the rights of citizenship itself. The Allotment Act was intended to extinguish all collective tribal ownership or stewardship of land by allotting individual Indians family-size farms. Any "surplus"

1. *Chief Joseph, Professor Edmond S. Meany, and Red Thunder, December 1903* (Curtis).

2. *Agent Albert M. Anderson and his family* (Avery). *This picture was probably taken in the summer of 1903, just before Anderson's dismissal from the Indian Service. It was made by Frank F. Avery, superintendent of schools on the Spokane Reservation and a keen amateur photographer.*

3. *Edward S. Curtis, c. 1905* (Muhr). *Adolf F. Muhr was the manager of Curtis' Seattle studio until his death in 1913. He used this portrait to illustrate a technical article he contributed to the West Coast photographic journal* Camera Craft *in 1906.*

4. *Dr. Edward H. Latham, summer 1901* (Avery).

5. *Professor Edmond S. Meany, c. 1905* (Prince).
Photographer George Prince ran a successful Seattle portrait studio.

6. *Steele's Hotel, Nespelem, c. 1901 (Latham). The white man wearing a tie in the center of the picture may be Henry Steele; the hotel became his by marriage in 1903.*

7. *Barnett Stillwell and daughter, Ada, summer 1901* (Meany).
The man in the background may be Henry Steele.

8. *Agent John McA. Webster (Avery). Captain Webster, in army uniform, poses with some of the chiefs and policemen of the Spokanes on the Spokane Reservation. On his left is Chief Oliver Lot; on his right, Chief William Three Mountains. He was agent for three reservations at the same time: Colville, Coeur d'Alene in Idaho, and Spokane.*

9. *The Columbia River, c. 1900* (Latham). *Much of the Colville Reservation is bounded by the Columbia. This view was probably made near the site of the present-day Chief Joseph Dam, which was built southwest of Nespelem in the 1950s.*

10. *Tepee circle, Fourth of July celebrations at Nespelem, 1900s* (Latham).

11. *Drummers, Fourth of July celebrations at Nespelem, 1900s* (Latham).
*This scene depicts some Nez Perces participating in what Agent Anderson called
"their primitive customs."*

12. *Nespelem, c. 1901 (Latham). In the 1890s the general store on the left was opened to provide supplies to white gold prospectors. On its roof is the sign of the post office which was opened in 1899.*

"Stage between Wilbur & Nespelem Wash".
Maj. Moorhouse

13. *The stage coach which ran from the railroad at Wilbur to Nespelem*
at the turn of the century (Moorhouse).

14. *Chief Joseph, c. 1901* (Moorhouse). *Lee Moorhouse was a very well-known and successful photographer of Northwest Indians. He lived at Pendleton, Oregon, and concentrated on views of the nearby Umatilla Reservation, of which he was also agent for a while. He first met Joseph on the Umatilla Reservation in 1890, and he visited Nespelem on at least one occasion before Joseph's death in 1904.*

15. *Chief Joseph's grave and monument, 1905* (Latham).

16. *The day school pupils and staff at Nespelem in 1903 (Moorhouse). The school had been closed in 1901 and Barnett Stillwell, the teacher, had moved to Lake Chelan. It was restarted and expanded a couple of years later, and was to experience further contractions, temporary closures, and enlargements in the first years of the twentieth century according to fluctuations in the Bureau of Indian Affairs educational policy and practice.*

reservation land was then opened to white settlement, the Indians receiving a token payment for the surplus land. Joseph's Nez Perces were barely settled at Nespelem when the Allotment Act came into force. His people were offered allotments near Lapwai on the Idaho Nez Perce Reservation but, because they still claimed lands in the Wallowa, most refused such titles. Some, however, did accept, including Chief Yellow Bull. Others took up allotments on the Colville Reservation but, since they were still unwilling and unable to farm them, they found it difficult to hold onto these plots and were in danger of becoming altogether landless.

Needless to say, real estate interests were strongly in favor of policies like the Allotment Act and in the case of the Colville Reservation there were extra incentives: good grazing land, much virgin forest, and—most alluring of all—gold. In 1891, with only the reluctant acquiescence of all the chiefs involved, the "North Half" of the reservation was opened up to white exploitation. Within a few short years Chief Joseph, Chief Moses, and others were to feel, as we shall see, that the "South Half" was threatened with a similar fate. Joseph was frequently placed in a situation in which he had to make representations on behalf of his people. He was clearly the undisputed leader of the Nez Perces, yet in normal circumstances he could not expect to see the undisputed leader of the Americans, the president. Usually, the best he could do was to visit the agent at agency headquarters at Chewelah (or, later, Miles), a good distance from Nespelem. More often than not, he would have to make a case to the subagent at Nespelem. (For many years Henry Steele held this position.) Whatever the issue, the subagent could rarely make a decision; he would send off a written request to the agent, and frequently, even on trivial matters, the agent would feel obliged to consult Washington, D.C. Consequently, literally nothing was easy to settle and time hung heavily on everyone, both Native Americans and the four or five Bureau employees at the subagency. There were endless petty squabbles among whites, among different tribes, between whites and Indians, between individuals of every description.

In a sense, Joseph and his people occupied a dimension of suspended time, always awaiting the major decision that they be allowed to return to the Wallowa Valley and usually awaiting the answers to numerous small inquiries. Meanwhile, the Nespelem of the white men was busily moving along linear time. The U.S. Indian Service employees—the farmer, the physician, the teacher, the sawyer, and the blacksmith—were joined by a storekeeper, then by another, then a hotel was built, and, finally, in 1899 a post office was established and Nespelem became a town. This was the world Edmond Meany entered when he came seeking biographical data on Chief Joseph in the summer of 1901. He had to travel about two hundred miles from Seattle as the crow flies. It was much further by train over the mighty Cascade Mountains, then by back-breaking wagon for a day from Wilbur to Nespelem, with a break for the ferry trip across the Columbia. And, in terms of differences in cultural values, the distance was much, much greater.

I do not know why Meany never completed the biography, and possibly the true reason would prove mundane—the pressures of teaching and endless organizing, the fleas of life, and so on—but in my fanciful explanation the cause has something to do with the subject himself, Chief Joseph. When I wrote the first draft of this book in 1977 it was the one hundredth anniversary of the flight, resistance, victories, and surrender of Joseph's people, and while in some senses a hundred years may seem a long time, it means that a number of the participants in those events survived well into the twentieth century. Not only could they leave memoirs to bridge the gap between them and us, but they were mostly barely a generation older than Meany and Curtis.

I think that when Meany and other regional historians of his era recorded a reminiscence or placed a monument to a recent incident they were aware that they were doing more than merely remembering something: they were isolating it from the flux of events; they were, in fact, *making* a history. And yet, in Joseph's case, despite the data—his own speeches, contemporary paintings, some letters transmitted through others, firsthand reports in newspapers and elsewhere, photographs, official documents—what we have is both more and less than a history.

Several of those Alvin Josephy has dubbed "the patriot chiefs" in his book of that title (1961)—Crazy Horse, Sitting Bull, and the Apache leader Geronimo are probably most suitable for purposes of comparison—loom large in the American consciousness as figures of *legend*. But their legends (as opposed to *them*, as human beings) are relatively simple and easy to read: Crazy Horse of the Oglala Sioux, mysterious in origin and motivation, clearly etched in victory at the Battle of the Little Big Horn in 1876, later murdered in shady circumstances and thus broken, eclipsed; Sitting Bull of the Hunkpapa Sioux, victorious but exiled, a mutterer brought home to die, also murdered. According to the facts, Geronimo's legend is somewhat closer to Joseph's in that he was also long in exile and, in a sense, lionized, but under closer scrutiny his is almost as simple as the others': one of savagery, or, at best, steadfast resistance, which becomes one of pathos, maybe even buffoonery, in the later images of him, being driven around a barren field, top hat askew, in an inappropriate automobile. Joseph's story, its meaning in the American consciousness, is so much more complex, a full remove more so, as to be different in kind.

It is clear from the first records of white contact with Joseph that from the start he always evoked an array of responses: some were won over by his calmness, charm, and pliability, while others thought him sullen and unbending. When war came he was immediately credited both with starting it (and was called a murderer) and with holding out for peace (and was considered weak). During the course of the war he was admired for skillful strategy and damned for the Nez Perce victories. In defeat he was reverenced for his eloquence but treated by the governing representatives of the people with respect and contempt in varying portions. His words possessed an uncanny resonance: "Tell General Howard I know his heart," he said, "Hear me, my chiefs! . . . From where the sun now stands I will fight no more forever." Or, "I learned [as a boy] that we were but few, while the white men were many. . . . We were like deer. They were like grizzly bears." Or, again, "The earth is the mother of all people, and all people should have equal rights upon it." He appealed to the tenets of a truly natural justice and to notions of equality similar to those on which the very constitution of the United States is supposed to rest. Yet, at the same time, he was known through his participation in the Nez Perce War as an enemy of those same United States. Contradictory currents of opinion were thus set in motion.

The Chronology that follows provides much of the primary data, extracts from speeches and the like, on which Joseph's complex fame rests. Suffice it to say at this point that throughout his long exile he suffered the abuse of disrespectful journalists and ill-educated settlers new to the Northwest, while his cause was taken up by thoughtful authors and others influential in the East. At the same time, in those whites closest to him towards his end a kaleidoscopic set of beliefs, passions, and prejudices is to be found; this may be seen in the letters of Steele and the others, which (with committed commentary, admittedly, but with a minimum of analysis) are reproduced as fully as possible here, primarily in the Narrative section of the book. I have tried to let each one speak for himself.

I have looked at much of the data available to Meany as Joseph's would-be biographer (together with some of his notes) and at many of the newspaper items in which he himself features. In my mental impression of him he works late into the night doing his historical accounts; he tears at his beard, but he knows that in Joseph's case the total will always be several figures too many or too few. They could not have come out just right. Because as well as being a man who could be met, held by the hand, weighed, and photographed, Chief Joseph of the Nez Perces was already a *myth*.

This book contains a couple of photographs of Chief Joseph's grave taken in 1905. The surroundings are bare, the newly erected monument almost glistens and the soil itself has a raw, freshly turned look. If today you visit the little cemetery where Joseph is buried—it is almost atop a low hill off a side road in Nespelem—there are many other Indian graves. Some are decorated with flowers and some have short poles topped with tinkling tinsel or bells to blow in the wind. Joseph's grave is nearly in the center of the plot. The earth over it has sunk down almost flat and the monument is somewhat weathered. But most noticeable of all is a small tree that grows beside the grave and bends over it, shading it from the full glare of the harsh sun and protecting it from the dusty fierceness of the Columbia Valley winds. In a similar way, our present-day vantage point on the Nez Perces and their chief is one more fully overarched by the myth of Joseph. This complex entity, however subtle, is, precisely by virtue of being a myth, static. So that when Curtis declares Joseph's head not the best to be found among the Nez Perces, or when Meany attempts to judge the chief by what he calls "the standards of the Indian" and "the standards of the white man," or, even, when Steele discovers it hard to understand his own unaccustomed grief over "the death of an Indian," the information they convey is less about Joseph than about themselves, their time, their culture. In other words, while Joseph as a flesh-and-blood human being certainly suffered more than his fair share of constraints in his later years—in that he suffered *both* those which all flesh seems heir to, such as failing physique and contradictory opinions, *and* those imposed specifically on him by an alien and mighty government—as a figure of myth he ultimately escapes such bonds of time and culture in a way that his witnesses do not. This is not to suggest that the array of attitudes exhibited by these whites, especially the assumption of racial superiority, is a thing only of the past, but rather to emphasize the degree to which the transcendent, the strangely untouched and untouchable nature of myth throws it into a kind of relief. Thus, the pattern I saw in the Meany collection and related materials was not one in which the bright light fell only on Joseph at the pivot, turning, but similarly on those at the perimeter of his path looking in, and also moving in their own seasons.

II. Chief Joseph of the Nez Perces

A CHRONOLOGY

tarting at the mouth of the Columbia, Coyote, who was a person of human form, led the salmon up the river as far as Waskopu (Celilo), where he found five women guarding a wall of stone across a stream. He opened a passage through this dam, led the fish through, and turned the five women into swallows. Then he continued up the river, leading the fish. At one place he called a salmon out of the water and began to roast it. While it was roasting, he fell asleep, and some people came and asked, "Old man, may we eat this?" He was snoring, and they [mistook his snores for an affirmative answer]. So they ate it. When Coyote awoke and found his fish gone, he was angry, but, knowing who had taken it, he vowed revenge. On Snake river, two days' journey above its mouth, he came upon a great many people lying around a fire. He turned them into beasts and birds of various kinds, and told them he was going to make people, and these animals should have pity on them and give them help when they went into the mountains to fast. [The people he made were the Nez Perces and this] was the beginning of the custom of fasting to obtain help from the spirits.[1]

c.1750   Wallowa Valley Nez Perces meet French trappers.

c.1786   Tu-eka-kas, later known as Joseph (Old Joseph), father of Chief Joseph, is born in the Wallowa Valley.

1805   *September 20*
          William Clark and others of the Lewis and Clark Expedition arrive in the Nez Perce homeland; starving, they are fed.

1812–13   Discord flares between American fur traders and the Nez Perces; the traders hang a Nez Perce boy for stealing.

1813–24   During a period of intertribal warfare made bloodier by the possession of newly acquired firearms, the Nez Perces trade with Canadian fur men.

1824–26   Trade and friendly relations between Nez Perces and Americans are reestablished.

1830   Influence of Christian missions begins among the Nez Perces.

1834   Fur trader Benjamin Bonneville is welcomed by the Nez Perces, including Tu-eka-kas.

1836   Henry and Eliza Spalding set up a Protestant mission station at Lapwai, Idaho, the first in the Nez Perce homeland; farming is adopted by some Nez Perces at Lapwai; disobedient or "insolent" Indians are whipped.

1838   Tu-eka-kas plants his tepee near the mission at Lapwai to hear the word of the white teachers and is given the name Joseph; in December he preaches to the Indians.

1839	Spalding, as Old Joseph's guest, becomes perhaps the first white to visit the Wallowa Valley Nez Perces in their own homeland; later in the year the chief is baptized into the Presbyterian Church.
1840	Hin-mah-too-yah-lat-kekt, known to the whites as Joseph, son of Old Joseph, is born in a cave near Joseph Creek.
1842	Dr. Elijah White, U.S. subagent to the Indians of Oregon, not yet a U.S. territory, coerces the Nez Perce chiefs gathered at Lapwai to accept a code of discipline he has devised and a single head chief, Ellis, to have authority over all the various bands.
1843	The first of many large wagon trains of American settlers to come overland annually to Oregon, near Nez Perce lands, arrives.
1845	Ellis, Lawyer, and some other chiefs, in their loyalty to the whites, are further divorced from their own people, who, fearing the increased numbers of immigrants, are becoming hostile to the missionaries.
1847	Cayuse Indians massacre the inmates of Marcus Whitman's Presbyterian mission at Waiilatpu in a peak of unrest due to the spread of the white man's diseases, increased settlement, resentment against the Whitmans personally, and Catholic and Protestant rivalry; Spalding's mission at Lapwai is attacked by a faction of the Nez Perce people and eventually closed.
1848	*Cayuse War* The Nez Perces, though opposed to American settlement, are divided and counsel peace with the whites. Nevertheless, the Nez Perce homeland is invaded by troops searching for the Cayuses responsible for the Whitman murders, and the occupation of Cayuse lands by whites serves notice to the Nez Perces that a similar fate could await them.
1850	Lawyer, who became head chief sometime after Ellis died of a measles epidemic on the Plains, agrees to urge the surrender of the guilty Cayuses. Five Cayuse leaders give themselves up and are executed.

The Nez Perce began his preparation for spiritual attainment almost in infancy. The child, either boy or girl, when less than ten years of age was told by the father or the mother that it was time to have tiwatitmas—spiritual power. "This afternoon you must go to yonder mountain and fast. When you reach the place of fasting, build a fire and do not let it die. As the Sun goes down, sit on the rocks facing him, watch while he goes from sight, and look in that direction all night. When the dawn comes, go to the east and watch the Sun return to his people. When he comes to noon, go to the south and sit there, and when he has travelled low again, go to the west where you sat first and watch until he is gone. Then start for your home." After some sacred object, such as a feather, had been tied to the child's clothing, and a few parting words of instruction and encouragement had been given, the little suppliant was sent on its journey. . . .

17. *A Nez Perce man, 1905, holding a heron's wing* (Curtis).

18. *A Nez Perce baby, 1900* (Curtis).
This portrait was probably made in Curtis' Seattle studio.

19. *A Cayuse woman, 1910* (Curtis). *Partly because of their proximity to the Whitman Mission, it was upon the Cayuse people that the first assertions of white dominance fell, and after their defeat in the Cayuse War they never regained their former strength or cohesiveness.*

20. *A Nez Perce sweat lodge, 1910* (Curtis). *Sweating was used to achieve physical and spiritual purification, as well as for mystical communion with the supernatural; it was a traditional custom much frowned upon by whites, especially agency physicians.*

21. *Watching for the signal, 1910* (Curtis). *Curtis frequently persuaded Indians to recreate scenes from the past for his camera.*

22. *A Nez Perce warrior, 1910* (Curtis).

23. *Chief Joseph in 1877* (Haynes). *This portrait, made in Bismarck, North Dakota, is the earliest known photograph of the Nez Perce leader. F. J. Haynes, an important pioneering photographer, became the official photographer for Yellowstone National Park.*

24. *Chief Joseph in Washington, D.C., 1879* (Jackson). *William Henry Jackson was a prominent early photographer of Indians and Western landscapes.*

For its first fasting a child was sent as far as from Lapwai to Lake
Waha, or to Taiya-mahsh, a mountain twelve miles to the south.
The child was familiar with the country and knew the trails because
the father had often talked to it and told it of the nature of the
land, pointing out the direction and saying that yonder was a place
of fasting. There was no ceremony or purification before setting out,
as the child was assumed to be pure. On ridges in the mountains
were places already prepared for the fasters, the makers now unknown,
as the monuments have been there time out of memory. They consist
of piles of stones about two feet high, arcs of circles, one with the
opening to the east, another open to the west, a third to the south.
Within these sat the faster, changing from one to the other as the
sun moved from east to west, and passing the night sleeplessly in
the western arc. He neither ate nor drank during the period of fasting,
which sometimes lasted two nights and a day.

As the time approached when the faster was expected to return,
the mother prepared a feast, and when the food was given to him it
was first blown upon by a medicine-man in order to purify it and
make it beneficial to the faster. All the family and the visitors ate
with him. He was not asked and did not tell of his vigil. Perhaps
the child a short time later was sent out again, either to the same
place or to a new one. Thus before reaching the age of fifteen he
might have been fasting in the mountains from five to ten times.[2]

1853   Washington Territory is established, its border with Oregon cutting the Nez Perce homeland into two parts.

1854–55   Governor Isaac Ingalls Stevens makes a series of treaties with coastal Washington Territory Indians which almost completely extinguish the Indians' right to their own lands. At a great council with the Nez Perce, Cayuse, Yakima, and other interior peoples he tries the same approach, but the chiefs, with the exception of Lawyer, sign half-heartedly in the belief that nothing will be activated for some years. Settlement starts immediately. War breaks out.

1856   Western Washington Indians are crushed.

1858   After a series of bloody skirmishes, including a massacre of Cayuses by Oregon irregulars in the Nez Perce homeland, and an uneasy peace, a regular army, riding to avenge the defeat of Lieutenant Colonel Edward J. Steptoe at the hands of Coeur D'Alenes and others, recruits pro-white elements from Lawyer's followers among the Nez Perces and embarks on a punitive mission against all the former allies of the Nez Perces in which several Indians are hung after surrendering.

1859   Stevens' treaty is ratified. Old Joseph, though no longer a Christian and trustful of whites, had signed it. On hearing of the ratification he says, "[The boundary of Nez Perce lands] was made as I wanted it, not for me but my children that will follow me. There [in the Wallowa Valley] is where I live and there is where I want to leave my body."[3]

1860   Gold is reported on Nez Perce lands. Although expressly forbidden by Stevens' treaties, almost overnight miners, merchants, and whole settlements appear. Lawyer's pro-white followers and many other Nez Perces accept the new developments, but they are opposed by others, including Old Joseph.

1861   A new agreement is made with Lawyer throwing some of the mining areas open to whites. The areas bordering the mines reserved for Indians are entered almost at once.

As a Nez Perce man passed through the forest the moving trees whispered to him and his heart swelled with the song of the swaying pine. He looked through the green branches and saw white clouds drifting across the blue dome, and he felt the song of the clouds. Each bird twittering in the branches, each water-fowl among the reeds or on the surface of the lake, spoke its intelligible message to his heart; and as he looked into the sky and saw the high-flying birds of passage, he knew that their flight was made strong by the uplifted voices of ten thousand birds of the meadow, forest, and lake, and his heart, fairly in tune with all this, vibrated with the songs of its fullness. Indians with a simple system in which the individual possessed only the spirit of the bird or the beast revealed to him are indeed close to nature, but the individual Nez Perce, with his interwoven devotional system, communed with almost unlimited nature.[4]

1863   Idaho Territory is created, its borders with Washington and Oregon cutting the Nez Perce homeland into three parts. Looking Glass, aged anti-treaty warrior chief, dies and is replaced by his son, also known as Looking Glass. A treaty council is held with the express purpose of reducing Nez Perce lands to a minimum; after suffering much browbeating and being offered inducements, the Christian and treaty bands under Lawyer sign the treaty. The non-treaty chiefs, including Old Joseph, White Bird, and Too-hool-hool-zote—who in the treaty are to lose their lands—refuse to sign and leave the council. The white commissioners nevertheless assert that the treaty has been made for all the Nez Perce nation.

1867   The 1863 treaty is ratified, but although the Nez Perces are forced to give up their lands in accordance with it, its provisions for the treaty bands are never fully met.

1871   Old Joseph dies and is buried in the Wallowa Valley not far from the confluence of the Wallowa and Lostine Rivers. Joseph assumes chieftainship of the Wallowa band.

1872   Settlers arrive in the Wallowa believing it open for settlement. Joseph calls a council to tell them to leave.

1873   In further treaty councils it is agreed, with the strength of a presidential decree, that Joseph's band can keep most of the Wallowa; white settlers are to be compensated for the loss of their recently acquired homesteads.

1874   Without informing Joseph, the Commissioner for Indian Affairs reverses the previous year's decree on the status of the Wallowa; as a result, more settlers pour in and tension builds. The non-treaty Indians hold two councils but agree not to fight.

1875   President Grant concurs with the Department of the Interior and rescinds his executive order of 1873. Joseph is informed, calls a council of non-treaty chiefs, but again decides not to fight, even though a wagon road for settlers is being laid into his valley. General Oliver Otis Howard, newly arrived army commander for the region, reports his belief that Joseph's band should be allowed to keep the Wallowa.

1876   Lawyer dies and is succeeded as head of the treaty chiefs by Reuben, Joseph's brother-in-law. In a dispute over some missing horses, two white settlers murder one of Joseph's band and the agent at Lapwai promises justice, but the courts fail to try the guilty man. Several times warriors under Joseph and his brother Ollokot dress for war to threaten the whites into leaving the Wallowa. Howard becomes convinced that Joseph's band is still legally entitled to the Wallowa Valley, but, since he accepts government policy, he advocates a council to extinguish Joseph's title, and stations troops in the valley as a buffer between whites and Indians. The commission, with Howard a member, is appointed.

1877   *January 6*

I have been talking to the whites for many years about the land in question, and it is strange they cannot understand me. The country they claim belonged to my father, and when he died it was given to me and my people, and I will not leave it until I am compelled to.[5] [Joseph to Agent John Monteith]

May
At the stormy council at Lapwai Joseph addresses Howard and the other commissioners:

The earth and myself are of one mind. The measure of the land and the measure of our bodies are the same. Say to us if you can say it that you were sent by the Creative Power to talk to us. Perhaps you think the Creator sent you here to dispose of us as you see fit.

If I thought you were sent by the Creator I might be induced to think you had a right to dispose of me. Do not misunderstand me, but understand me fully with reference to my affection for the land. I never said the land was mine to do with as I chose. The one who has the right to dispose of it is the one who has created it. I claim the right to live on my land, and accord you the privilege to live on yours.[6]

During the course of the council, troops are brought up to cover Joseph's people in the Wallowa and Too-hool-hool-zote is thrown into the guardhouse; the non-treaty Nez Perces are cowed into submission.

May 14
Howard gives the non-treaties thirty days to get onto the Idaho reservation at Lapwai. A day's ride from the reservation—after packing belongings, fearful crossings of swollen rivers and consequent loss of livestock—they gather for a final meeting in freedom. Two of White Bird's band, smarting from past indignities, decide to seek personal vengeance; in a foray back to their own Salmon River country they kill several whites known to them as Indian haters. Tension builds into a general outbreak of violence; Joseph and his Wallowa band cannot avoid war along with most, though not all (Looking Glass' band keeps away), of the other non-treaty bands. In the fighting that will inevitably follow Joseph undoubtedly contributes to the group strategy, but he is not considered a war leader like Too-hool-hool-zote, and is usually assigned the logistical task of leading the old, the women and children, and the infirm to safety.

1877   WAR

June 17: White Bird Battle
The Nez Perce leaders send out a white flag of truce to Captain David Perry. When it is ignored, they attack his troop in White Bird Canyon, disorganizing, then routing him.

July 1: Attack on Looking Glass' Village
At dawn regular troops and Idaho volunteers under Captain Stephen C. Whipple ignore an emissary sent out from Looking Glass under a white flag; despite the peaceful intentions of his band, the village is attacked. The troops shoot, destroy property, and loot at random. Looking Glass joins the war.

July 2: Rains' Defeat
Whipple sends out a scouting detachment of thirteen men under Lieutenant Sevier M. Rains. A small group of Nez Perces destroy them.

July 4–5: Cottonwood Skirmish

A Nez Perce decoy party attacks a group of volunteers on their way to join the contained forces of Whipple and Perry at Cottonwood. The Nez Perces suffer the loss of one of their warriors and withdraw, the mass of the people having meanwhile by-passed the Gatling guns being brought up to destroy them.

July 11–12: Battle of Clearwater

The Nez Perces pen down a regiment of irregulars, take their horses, and let them drift away, defeated. But while their attention is thus distracted, Howard's own troop, having been fruitlessly in pursuit of them for two weeks, comes upon their camp from another direction and attacks it with artillery. Too-hool-hool-zote and a small band of warriors hold their advance while the main mass organizes, regroups and its approximately 200 men hold off Howard's 560-man army for two days. The Nez Perces withdraw after Howard receives reinforcements and announces a victory.

July 15

Looking Glass urges escape to Montana and their friends on the Plains, the Crows. It is agreed and Looking Glass becomes supreme war leader. The next day the non-treaty Nez Perces leave their homeland.

July 28

After peace discussions between Captain Charles C. Rawn and Looking Glass on the Lolo Trail, the Nez Perces successfully evade a battle and enter settled areas of Montana, broadcasting their peaceful intentions to the whites.

August 9: Big Hole Battle

Looking Glass and the people, overconfident and relaxed, are attacked in the camps by a large force of regular troops and Montana volunteers under General John Gibbon. Many Nez Perce lives—mostly women and children—are lost in the initial confusion. Joseph and White Bird outflank the troops and lead the families to safety while the warriors under Ollokot and Looking Glass split Gibbon's force; in an attempt to regroup, the army is held in a siege position all day by the Nez Perces. Gradually the warriors break off the engagement to give protection to the fleeing and mourning families. Poker Joe, deeply familiar with the buffalo country, is appointed guide and war leader.

August 20: Camas Meadows Fight

A Nez Perce war party under Ollokot and Looking Glass stampedes Howard's pack animals (and holds off its pursuers), further slowing the already tortuous progress of Howard's army. Random attacks on settlers, in revenge for the dawn charge on their camp at Big Hole, alarm the U.S. authorities and a network of armies rings the newly defined Yellowstone National Park ready to attack the Indians wherever and whenever they emerge.

September 13: Battle of Canyon Creek
The Nez Perces outwit the army, passing out of the National Park almost under the nose of Colonel Samuel D. Sturgis, who then gives chase. They are caught entering Canyon Creek, but the warriors, firing from cover at the mouth of the canyon, successfully hold back an army advance on their families, inflicting heavy casualties on an ill-advised cavalry charge.

September 15
Disillusioned, the Nez Perce warriors, under Ollokot, are forced into fights with Indian scouts working for the army, including their former allies, the Crows. The plains country is clearly unsafe for the non-treaty Nez Perces, and they decide to move northwards to join Sitting Bull's non-treaty Sioux in exile in Canada.

September 23: Cow Island Fight
In order to steal food supplies, the fleeing Nez Perces carry out a desultory attack against a small detachment of troops guarding stores. They are weary and discouraged. Looking Glass, knowing that Howard is far behind and ignorant of the new army under Colonel Nelson A. Miles advancing to intercept them, retakes command from Poker Joe and orders a slower pace.

September 30–October 5: Bear Paws Battle
Only forty miles from Canada and freedom, with winter approaching, the Nez Perce camp is charged by Miles' army. In the first rush of confused and vicious fighting casualties on both sides are heavy; the Indians lose Ollokot, Too-hool-hool-zote and Poker Joe. Sporadic fire is exchanged as snow descends over the battlefield. Under a flag of truce Miles calls for talks with Joseph. Joseph refuses to surrender and, in a violation of the truce, Joseph is detained in Miles' camp. The Indians retaliate by holding Lieutenant Lovell H. Jerome in their camp. Fighting continues under driving snow, the army now also using a cannon, and two days later Joseph and Jerome are exchanged. On October 4, with the people hungry and cold, they are shocked when a cannon shell lands directly in a dugout shelter killing a small girl and her grandmother. On October 5, Howard having arrived, two treaty Nez Perces are sent to Joseph with terms for the Nez Perce surrender: give up and you can return to the Northwest in peace. The Indians hold a council. Afterwards, showing himself

too precipitantly, Looking Glass is fired on and killed. Joseph is again assured by Miles that they will be allowed to return "home." Feeling that he can do so with honor, Joseph tells the people he will surrender, and does so:

Tell General Howard I know his heart. What he told me before, I have it in my heart. I am tired of fighting. Our chiefs are killed. Looking Glass is dead. Too-hool-hool-zote is dead. The old men are all dead. It is the young men who say, "Yes" or "No." He who led the young men is dead. It is cold, and we have no blankets. The little children are freezing to death. My people, some of them, have run away to the hills, and have no blankets, no food. No one knows where they are, perhaps freezing to death. I want to have time to look for my children, and see how many of them I can find. Maybe I shall find them among the dead. Hear me, my chiefs! I am tired. My heart is sick and sad. From where the sun now stands I will fight no more forever.[7]

With Joseph in surrender are 86 men, 184 women, and 147 children; these are fed and warmed at the soldiers' fires, then transported to Fort Keogh and captivity. Distrustful of Howard, White Bird secretly leads a party of perhaps two hundred refugees as swiftly as possible from the battlefield; starving, they reach Canada and are fed and protected by Sitting Bull's people.

November 1
Despite his strong feeling that his own and Howard's pledge that the Nez Perces could return to the Northwest should be honored, Miles is ordered to take his prisoners further south, to Fort Lincoln, near Bismarck, North Dakota.

November 16
Joseph's people, bedraggled and bowed down, arrive in Bismarck. Joseph is photographed. Miles again tries to help; he asks permission to bring Joseph to Washington, D.C., but he is refused.

November 27
The Nez Perces arrive by train at Fort Leavenworth, Kansas, and are forced to camp there, in insanitary conditions, indefinitely.

December 10
Joseph sends a petition to Washington, asking to be allowed to return to the Northwest. It is ignored.

1878   *July*
With over twenty people already dead and the rest ridden with malaria, Joseph and his people are moved to the Quapaw Reservation

in Kansas Territory. Here nearly fifty more die by the end of the year.

1879   *January*
Joseph and Yellow Bull visit the capital to plead their case with President Rutherford B. Hayes and Congress.

April
Joseph publishes his argument in "An Indian's View of Indian Affairs" in *The North American Review*, saying, in part:

I want the white people to understand my people. Some of you think an Indian is like a wild animal. This is a great mistake. I will tell you about our people, and then you can judge whether an Indian is a man or not. I believe much trouble and blood would be saved if we opened our hearts more. . . .

[On his deathbed my father said:] "My son, never forget my dying words. This country holds your father's body. Never sell the bones of your father and your mother." I pressed my father's hand and told him that I would protect his grave with my life. My father smiled and passed away to the spiritland.

I buried him in that beautiful valley of winding waters. I love that land more than all the rest of the world. A man who would not love his father's grave is worse than a wild animal. . . .

In the treaty councils the commissioners have claimed that our country had been sold to the Government. Suppose a white man should come to me and say, "Joseph, I like your horses, and I want to buy them." I say to him, "No, my horses suit me, I will not sell them." Then he goes to my neighbor, and says to him: "Joseph has some good horses. I want to buy them, but he refuses to sell." My neighbor answers, "Pay me the money, and I will sell you Joseph's horses." The white man returns to me and says, "Joseph, I have bought your horses, and you must let me have them." If we sold our lands to the Government, this is the way they were bought. . . .

I have carried a heavy load on my back ever since I was a boy. I learned then that we were but few, while the white men were many, and that we could not hold our own with them. We were like deer. They were like grizzly bears. We had a small country. Their country was large. We were contented to let things remain as the Great Spirit Chief made them. They were not; and would change the rivers and mountains if they did not suit them. . . .

[For the coming of war] I blame my young men and I blame the white men. I blame General Howard for not giving my people time to get their stock away from Wallowa. I do not acknowledge that he had the right to order me to leave Wallowa at any time. I deny

that either my father or myself ever sold that land. It is still our land. It may never again be our home, but my father sleeps there, and I love it as I love my mother. I left there, hoping to avoid bloodshed. . . .

[Since the war I have been pleading to be allowed to return to the Northwest.] At last I was granted permission to come to Washington and bring my friend Yellow Bull and our interpreter with me. I am glad we came. I have shaken hands with a great many friends, but there are some things I want to know which no one seems able to explain. I cannot understand how the Government sends a man out to fight us, as it did General Miles, and then breaks his word. Such a Government has something wrong about it. I cannot understand why so many chiefs are allowed to talk so many different ways, and promise so many different things. I have seen the Great Father Chief (the President); the next Great Chief (Secretary of the Interior); the Commissioner Chief (Hayt); the Law Chief (General Butler), and many other law chiefs (Congressmen), and they all say they are my friends, and that I shall have justice, but while their mouths all talk right I do not understand why nothing is done for my people. I have heard talk and talk, but nothing is done. Good words do not last long until they amount to something. Words do not pay for my dead people. They do not pay for my country, now overrun by white men. They do not protect my father's grave. They do not pay for my horses and cattle. Good words will not make good the promise of your War Chief, General Miles. Good words will not give my people good health and stop them from dying. Good words will not get my people a home where they can live in peace and take care of themselves. I am tired of talk that comes to nothing. It makes my heart sick when I remember all the good words and all the broken promises. There has been too much talking by men who had no right to talk. Too many misrepresentations have been made, too many misunderstandings have come up between the white men about the Indians. If the white man wants to live in peace with the Indian he can live in peace. There need be no trouble. Treat all men alike. Give them all the same law. Give them all an even chance to live and grow. All men were made by the Great Spirit Chief. They are all brothers. The earth is the mother of all people, and all people should have equal rights upon it. You might as well expect the rivers to run backward as that any man who was born a free man should be contented penned up and denied liberty to go where he pleases. If you tie a horse to a stake, do you expect he will grow fat? If you pen an Indian up on a small spot of earth, and compel him to stay there, he will not be contented nor will he grow and prosper. I have asked some of the great white chiefs where they get their authority to say to the Indian

that he shall stay in one place, while he sees white men going where they please. They cannot tell me.

I only ask of the Government to be treated as all other men are treated. If I cannot go to my own home, let me have a home in some country where my people will not die so fast. I would like to go to Bitter Root Valley. There my people would be healthy; where they are now they are dying. Three have died since I left my camp to come to Washington.

When I think of our condition my heart is heavy. I see men of my race treated as outlaws and driven from country to country, or shot down like animals.

I know that my race must change. We cannot hold our own with the white men as we are. We only ask an even chance to live as other men live. We ask to be recognized as men. We ask that the same law shall work alike on all men. If the Indian breaks the law, punish him by the law. If the white man breaks the law, punish him also.

Let me be a free man—free to travel, free to stop, free to work, free to trade, where I choose, free to choose my own teachers, free to follow the religion of my fathers, free to think and talk and act for myself—and I will obey every law, or submit to the penalty.

Whenever the white man treats the Indian as they treat each other, then we shall have no more wars. We shall be all alike—brothers of one father and one mother, with one sky above us and one country around us, and one government for all. Then the Great Spirit Chief who rules above will smile upon this land, and send rain to wash out the bloody spots made by brothers' hands upon the face of the earth. For this time the Indian race are waiting and praying. I hope that no more groans of wounded men and women will ever go to the ear of the Great Spirit Chief above, and that all people may be one people.

In-mut-too-yah-lat-lat has spoken for his people.

Young Joseph[8]

June
The Nez Perces are moved to a new camp on the Ponca Reservation in Indian Territory, Oklahoma. But the people are still dying, especially newborn babies and children (including one of Joseph's daughters). Three Christian Nez Perces, including James Reuben, come to act as teachers to the exiles.

1881   General Howard publishes *Nez Perce Joseph,* an account of *his ancestors, his lands, his confederates, his enemies, his murders, his war, his pursuit and capture.* Miles again appeals for Joseph's band to be allowed to return to the Northwest. In his report of September, the agent at the Ponca Reservation asks for the relocation to Idaho of "the surplus women" caused by the war.

1883   James Reuben is granted permission to take twenty old men, women, and orphans to the Lapwai Reservation.

1885   The 268 survivors of the non-treaty bands taken into captivity are allowed to return to the Northwest. About half of them are housed at Lapwai. But Joseph's Wallowa band is sent first to the agency headquarters at Chewelah, then to Nespelem on the Colville Reservation in eastern Washington. Joseph's people are not welcomed by some of the tribes already domiciled at and near Nespelem, and troops are called in to settle the Nez Perces.

1886   Old Joseph's grave is desecrated, his skull put on exhibition.

1889   The remaining reservation land at Lapwai is divided into separate allotments for Indians to claim individually, and Joseph's people are given the opportunity to take up such allotments. Joseph refuses, still claiming his own lands in the Wallowa. His friend Yellow Bull accepts, and moves in 1891. Joseph visits the city of Portland, Oregon, to sit for a bas-relief plaque of his head by Olin L. Warner; the artist has been commissioned by Colonel C. E. S. Wood, Howard's former aide, now a lawyer interested in Joseph's case.

1891   About half, the "North Half," of the enormous Colville Reservation is opened up to settlement by whites; most of the various tribes reluctantly sign the treaty of agreement.

1892   Joseph is visited for five months by Colonel Wood's son, Erskine, a thirteen-year-old boy.

1893   Joseph again receives a summer visit from Erskine Wood.

1896   Joseph, together with Chief Moses of the Columbias, vigorously opposes the opening of a day school for the children of Nez Perce and Columbia families at Nespelem. When the school opens, they at first discourage attendance.

1897   White miners encroach onto the "South Half" of the Colville Reservation. Fearing disturbances, Joseph travels to Washington, D.C. to complain. He renews his claim to the Wallowa Valley and receives some support from General Miles. In New York, in company with Generals Howard and Miles, Joseph participates in the dedication parade to the tomb of Grant, the President whose change of policy had allowed him to be ousted from the Wallowa. As a guest of "Buffalo Bill" Cody, he stays at the Astor House. The Bureau of Indian Affairs promises to investigate Joseph's case.

1899   *June 6*
         At the opening of a potlatch ceremony to commemorate the passing of Chief Moses, Joseph is presented with a suit of buckskin and a headdress that had been given to Moses by Sitting Bull. Holding high the war-bonnet, he speaks thus:

Friends, we are gathered here today in accordance with an Indian custom that is very old. We, friends of the great chief, who had not seen the breath leave his body, have searched for him diligently in his usual haunts. We have not found him, so we must accept the statement of his relatives that he has passed away. Passed away like the glory of the Indian that is represented by this war-bonnet, now given to my keeping; passed away like the health and vigor of our Northwestern Indians; passed away as we all must some day—men and women, old and young. . . . This beautiful war-bonnet given into my keeping shall be carefully preserved, and it shall be honored with the best place in my house. For the sake of him I revered in life on this earth, I shall honor this emblem—whose owner is not dead, but only passed away to the Great Spirit that we now know not.[9]

Joseph visits the Wallowa for the first time since the war, but at a public meeting of whites he is told that he and his people will not be sold land for a reservation anywhere in the valley.

1900 On August 24, through the hand of Barnett Stillwell, U.S. Indian School Service teacher at Nespelem, Joseph communicates with Professor Edmond S. Meany:

Nespelem, Wash,
August 24—1900,

Edmond L. Meany
Seattle University, Wash,

Dear Sir:

Your favor of the 7th inst. from Madison, Wis. came to hand a few days ago. I have just returned from Wallowa where I went with Inspector [James] McLaughlin to look over my old home and see if I could find a new home now. There are many white people there now, but I told the inspector I would be satisfied with some land on one side of the river where there were only a few whites, and where creeks and mountains afforded good pasturage. I would be happy with very little.

You would be very welcome here. I would be glad to see you. A long time ago we were not friends to the white people but we are friends now. I would be glad to hear from you again.

My father, mother and brother are buried at Wallowa and when I die I want to be buried there.

When I went to Washington everybody was kind to me and I thought that very nice.

The Inspector told me he would write to me when he got back

*to Washington but I do not hear from him. He was going to report
and then write and tell me the decision.*

*I like your letter very much. I will be pleased to hear from you
again.*

Very Truly Yours,
Chief Joseph

1901   In a letter to Meany of May 27, 1901, written in Barnett Stillwell's
hand, Joseph agrees to a visit by Edmond Meany, saying in part:

*Dear Sir: Replying to your favor of the 20th inst. I am in good health
and was very glad to hear from you. You are probably aware that I
lost my children years ago. The children of my people are attending
the Day School on the reservation and I feel very kindly to the school.
This land belonged to the late Chief Moses. It does not belong to
me. My old home is in the Wallowa Valley and I want to go back
there to live. My father and mother are buried there. If the Government
would only give me a small piece of land for my people in the Wallowa
Valley with a teacher that is all I would ask. I am glad to hear of
your proposed trip to this place and will welcome you.*

Joseph is visited by Meany in June. Later in the year he is informed
that the Commissioner does not favor the return of his people to
Oregon.

1902   A bill is introduced in Congress for the relief of Joseph's people by
payment of sums due to them as a result of the sale of lands formerly
occupied by them in Indian Territory. Such relief is contested by
the Bureau of Indian Affairs.

1903   Joseph again visits Washington, D.C., as Miles' guest. He also stays
in New York City to participate in various Western events.

November 20
Joseph delivers a speech in a Seattle theater:

My White Friends:—
*I am pleased to meet you all this evening, old and young. I feel
very thankful for such a kind and hearty reception in your city. I
have a kind feeling in my heart for you all. I am getting old and for
some years past, have made several efforts to be returned to my old
home in Wallo-wa Valley, but without success. The Government at
Washington has always given me many flattering promises but up
to the present time has utterly failed to fulfill any of its promises to
me. But I am not surprised as much of my life has been filled with
broken promises. I have but few years to live and would like to die*

in my old home. My father is buried there, my children are buried there and I would like to rest by their side when I die. I have fought bravely and honorably in defending my inheritance from [the Creative Power]—the land and houses of my forefathers. I will fight no more and hope you will all help me to return to the home of my childhood where my relatives and friends are resting. Please assist me. I am thankful for your kind attention. That is all.[10]

November 11
While in Seattle Joseph is also prevailed upon to address the students at the University of Washington, and says:

My Young Friends:—

I am pleased to meet you all and glad to see so many present. It always gives me pleasure to meet my white friends, I seem to have so many more now, than during my younger life. I am an Indian but the same blood that courses through my veins flows through yours. I was born and reared [to lead] the free, open and unrestricted life of a brave and haughty warrior. When I reached manhood I found that conditions were rapidly changing and without going into details, fought for my people, my land and my home. I fought for the inheritance left me by my forefathers and given me by [the Creator]. I was vanquished, conquered and subjugated, and have keenly felt the humiliation of defeat. But I have come to fully realize the kindness and generosity of the whites. I now see that they are my friends.

In my declining years, I long to return to my old home in Wallowa Valley, where most of my relatives and friends are sleeping their last sleep. I have repeatedly petitioned the Great Father in Washington to transfer my self and small band to our old home, that we may die in the Country, having so many tender memories. I have made frequent visits to Washington and have met many persons high in official life. They have all promised to render their assistance, but it has been, wait, wait, wait. On my last visit to the Capital City, I had the honor and pleasure of meeting President Roosevelt who treated me with much kind consideration. He assured me that a committee would be sent out to investigate my condition and surroundings. This committee was to be at my home last July but they have not yet come. This is but one instance of the duplicity shown me by the Government. I hope you will all help me and render me what assistance you can in securing long delayed justice. To return to Wallowa Valley, is a wish I Cherish very dearly. That is all.[11]

1904   In the spring Joseph attends the commencement exercises at Carlisle Indian Industrial School, Pennsylvania and is seated at a banquet table with General Howard. Joseph says, in part:

Friends, I meet here my friend, General Howard. I used to be anxious to meet him. I wanted to kill him in war. Today I am glad to meet him, . . . and to be friends with General Howard. We are both old men, still we live and I am glad.[12]

Joseph travels on to the St. Louis Exposition and returns to Nespelem in time for the annual July Fourth celebrations.

September 21
Joseph dies.

1905   *June 20*
Joseph is reburied at Nespelem and a monument erected to his memory. Yellow Bull, in the course of the ceremonies, speaks:

I am glad to see our white friends here attending this ceremony, and it seems . . . we all have the same sad feelings, and [this should] wipe [away] my tears. Joseph is dead, but his words are not dead; his words will live forever. This monument will stand—and Joseph's words will stand as long as this monument. . . .[13]

III. White Witnesses to Chief Joseph's End

A NARRATIVE

I N 1898 Edmond S. Meany was already a prominent figure in the Pacific Northwest: a prolific writer for local newspapers, a former legislator, and a perennial booster of the State of Washington. He was also already professor of history at the University of Washington, so he felt piqued and stung personally by some remarks made by President David Starr Jordan of Stanford University. In a much-quoted Seattle speech, Jordan had inveighed against the poor academic qualifications of some West Coast professors. Virtually as a direct response, Meany (who had once been taught by Jordan) enrolled as a part-time candidate for the degree of Master of Letters at the University of Wisconsin. Wisconsin was a most prestigious institution for history at that time and Meany's own faculty advisers were the prominent theoretician of the frontier, Frederick Jackson Turner, and the controversial political economist, Richard T. Ely. He also came under the influence of Reuben Gold Thwaites, who was gathering prodigious collections of pioneer memoirs and data at the library of the Wisconsin State Historical Society in Madison. The subject of Meany's thesis, probably suggested by Turner, was to be Chief Joseph. At that time, Joseph was residing within the boundaries of Meany's own adopted state—in exile, he himself claimed, and virtually a prisoner of war—at Nespelem.

Fellow historian Max Farrand once wrote to Meany that "Turner always said you were a hustler,"[1] and certainly in this case Meany set about his task with a vigor that would be the envy of most people but that was simply characteristic for him. He wrote a barrage of letters to the great ones of the time soliciting their opinions on Joseph's significance; he received replies from, among others, Theodore Roosevelt and "Buffalo Bill" Cody. Roosevelt, perhaps untypically, was relatively tentative:

I am sure you will sympathize with my feeling that a man should not give a kind of snap shot historic judgment. I have not studied the life of Chief Joseph with sufficient closeness to entitle me to pass upon him a judgment which I should be willing to have quoted as my final and deliberate opinion. It is fair to say, however, that [from] what I have read and heard of his exploits and his character . . . from [others] I feel that he was a noteworthy man, and I am glad that you are making a study of him.[2]

Cody, as usual, had no reservations; "I consider Chief Joseph—the Nez Perce Chief—the greatest Indian America ever produced," he declared.[3]

Meany also wrote several times to the Bureau of Indian Affairs, to the Smithsonian's Bureau of American Ethnology, and to other possible sources of evidence and opinion, including Joseph's captor, General Nelson A. Miles. As the bibliography to Meany's thesis attests, he read the official documentation of U.S. relations with the Nez Perces, the relevant periodical literature, and the book-length memoirs of various participants. But as well as studying in the libraries of Seattle and Madison, he also devoted the week of June 31, 1901 to visiting, in person, the Nespelem Nez Perces. While there he became acquainted with Edward

H. Latham, the agency physician; Barnett Stillwell, the teacher; and Henry
M. Steele, the subagent and farmer.

Meany's visit cost him $33.50 all told, if presents, cigars, and a $6.00 payment
to Chief Joseph are included. He entered these figures in a notebook he kept
of his days at Nespelem in which he also recorded such matters as the shape
of Joseph's horse brand, a statement signed by Henry Steele and himself to
the effect that Joseph conferred upon him the name of Three Knives on June
26, and notes on both his new white acquaintances and on Joseph. Joseph
told him that he acquired his name—which in translation means, roughly, "Thunder in the Mountains"—from the substance of a vision he experienced during
a vigil in the mountains near his boyhood home in the Wallowa. Undaunted
collector that Meany was, he got the chief to write his signature for him and
attached to it a formal statement signed by Barnett and Dema Stillwell and
himself:

*Nespilem, Colville Reservation, Washington, 25 VI, 1901. We, the undersigned,
witnessed Chief Joseph copy the above signature using the signature under the
frontispiece of General O. O. Howard's book entitled "Chief Joseph, the Nez
Perce, His Pursuit and Capture" as a guide.*[4]

As an historian, Meany's primary concern during his visit was, of course, to
gather as much information as possible on Joseph's part in the war of 1877
and in the events that led up to it; his notebook documents Joseph's answers,
and the manner of his answers, to a number of questions Meany plied him
with. In his resulting thesis, "Chief Joseph, the Nez Perce," Meany disentangled
the web of treaties and penetrated the complex of changing allegiances among
the Indians and the bungling and greed among the whites with assurance, precision, and verve. But Meany, like Turner, his teacher, was also profoundly concerned with the frontier of his own immediate period: he got a statement from
Joseph, in the hand of Barnett Stillwell, dated June 25, 1901, which outlined
the current plight of the Nez Perces, and the last chapter of his dissertation
was in fact called "Present Conditions."

Moreover, while Meany was essentially conservative, a traditionalist, and a
believer in America's "manifest destiny," he had a genuine, if paternalistic,
interest in Indian welfare, both generally and with reference to specific individuals. His correspondence during this period testifies to his support of the efforts
of the agent at the Tulalip Reservation, Charles M. Buchanan, in his struggle
to get a larger appropriation of funds for his school; it also reveals his interest
in the case of Luke Hobucket, a policeman on the Quilliute Reservation who
had been wrongly threatened with dismissal as a result of factional disagreements
among his own people. Since Meany was not a man who shied away from
controversy, it is not surprising that, like General Miles and others, he was
prepared to support Joseph on the question of the rightful home for the aging
chief and his band. Meany was definitely in receipt of the most recent of the

lengthy and legalistic reports of the Bureau of Indian Affairs. This BIA submission stated the case against Joseph very forcefully, but in his dissertation Meany reached his own conclusions:

The Colville Reservation has been cut in two. The Government has thus far neglected to pay the Indians the $1,500,000 agreed upon for the northern half. The southern half has also been thrown open for mineral entries and the familiar haunts and pasture lands of the Indians are now being overrun by a constant stream of prospectors. The writer visited one mining camp within two miles of Chief Joseph's tepee where the herds of Indian ponies are startled twice a day by the blasting of the rocks. At the sub-agency are two stores where these miners procure supplies. . . .

Chief Moses of the Columbians had been located on the Nespilem before Chief Joseph's band was brought there. He had gone to Washington City and secured many favors for his people such as a saw-mill, grist-mill, physician, blacksmith and school and a yearly salary for himself of one thousand dollars. He also procured certain allowances of agricultural implements.

Chief Joseph got no salary but the Government has issued his people regular rations of food, clothes and agricultural implements. From this fact and from the fact that he and the members of his band are supposed to ask permission if they wish to leave the reservation it is construed that Joseph's band are still practically prisoners of war.

The best agriculturalists in this vicinity are the remnants of the original Nespilems, who first occupied the land. They live in frame houses, till the soil and, with unusual pride, refuse to receive aid from the Government. If they got a reaper from the Government store-house they insist on paying for it in hay or labor.

Joseph's band, on the other hand, being supplied with everything they need, do not progress in the industrial activities. It is claimed that this idleness is a bad influence on the other Indians and the agents have been asking the Government to curtail and finally discontinue all rations to the Nez Perces.

In order to get lumber for houses, barns or other purposes, the Indians go to the hills and cut the logs, which they haul to the mill. Then they assist the Government sawyer to cut the logs into whatever shape is desired. They mark their own logs and keep track of all the details carrying the finished product in their homes.

The Government built for Chief Joseph, a small, rough-board, battened house and a barn on the farm he selected about four miles from the sub-agency. The Chief will not live in his house and the roof of his barn is broken in. He prefers to live in the traditional tepee, winter and summer, and this tepee he has pitched near the sub-agency so he can be near his people and the school.

The teacher of the school, Barnett Stillwell, who has been there for four years, says that Chief Joseph has manifested great interest in the children. He often visits the school, at which times the Indian children would remain almost motion-

less. On several occasions he administered light punishment to some of the little ones, who were not progressing to suit him.

Not far from the school house is the Nez Perce burial ground. The headstones consist of poles set in the ground with bells or feathers ornamenting the tops. It forms a weird picture of mingled savagery and civilization. Chief Joseph presides at every Nez Perce funeral with great and solemn dignity.

The interior of Chief Joseph's tepee presents a model appearance of neatness. Indian mats cover the floor and in huge rolls around the edge are buffalo robes now quite scarce among the Indians, and blankets. From one of these rolls the Chief brought a small leather trunk in which were bundles of letters he had received from white men, and photographs of Indian and white friends. He knew each face and seemed glad to call up memories of his friends and relatives. At the bottom of his trunk were the eagle hat and saddle robe with which his high rank is proclaimed on all gala days.

The Indians were making great preparations for the approaching Fourth of July when they would have a celebration extending over one or two weeks. Joseph would not allow his picture to be taken until that time when his wardrobe would be in a better condition for such an important operation. The Indians of this whole region show their respect for Chief Joseph by according him, without any questioning, the principal place of honor on all great festivals or celebrations.

Chief Moses had a great reputation among the Indians and whites of this section but he was dissipated. The Indians will manage at times to get liquor and Moses brought on his own death by a protracted spree. Chief Joseph never drinks intoxicants. "Nica Halo Bottlum," as he puts it in Chinook (meaning, "I never touch the bottle").

Moses had two wives who survive him. Joseph is now the only Indian on the reservation who has two wives. His wives are Wa-win-te-pi-ksat, aged forty-six, and I-a-tu-ton-my, aged thirty-nine. Joseph's Nez Perce name is Hin-mah-too-ya-lat-kekht meaning "Thunder rolling in the mountains." He claims that he is fifty-three years old but General Howard estimated his age at thirty-seven at the time of his war, which would make him sixty-one years old now.

Henry M. Steele, the sub-agent at Nespilem, says that Joseph's wives do all the work about the home and always call for the rations on issue day. He says that Joseph is appealed to when there are harnesses or other such goods to give out to the Nez Perces. The Chief will designate the ones to be thus favored but he usually begins the process by claiming one of the articles for himself.

On our visits to the tepee, the writer saw Joseph unharnessing his team and on another day he was saddling a pony. The sub-agent said on both occasions that it was unusual. The wives or his helpers usually did such things for him.

The Government has built for Joseph two small "ietas," houses in which are kept his many precious properties. In one are four rifles. One of these is old and worn. Joseph says it is the one he carried through the war. Here is also seen nicely framed the certificate of Chief Joseph's appointment as an aid in the New York parade at the dedication of the Grant memorial monument on

April 27, 1897. On that occasion he marched side by side with his friend Buffalo Bill.

Joseph was asked what Indian chiefs he considered the greatest and he answered that he thought his father, also a Chief Joseph, was the greatest. To another question he said he thought his brother Ollicutt was the next greatest chief.

Joseph has had nine children, five girls and four boys, but they are all dead. One died since living at Nespilem, two died in Indian Territory and the rest died in Idaho. One daughter grew to womanhood and was married. He seems especially fond of her memory and tells what a good girl she was while showing her picture. On the back of this tintype picture is written "for Chief Joseph from his loving Daughter Sarah Moses."

Bereft of his children the Chief now leads a quiet life sustained by the Government against whose authority he waged a long and bitter warfare. His last effort to regain the Wallowa Valley has been investigated by Inspector James McLaughlin who has reported strongly against the request. But Joseph still longs for that old home the "Valley of Winding Waters." In a dictated letter to the writer, dated at Nespilem, May 27, 1901, he says: "My old home is in the Wallowa Valley and I want to go back there to live. My father and mother are buried there. If the Government would only give me a small piece of land for my people in the Wallowa Valley, with a teacher, that is all I would ask."

The white people in Wallowa Valley have named one of their towns Joseph and their newspaper was called Chieftain but there the sentiment ends. They enter strong protest when it is talked of sending any of the Nez Perces back to that home of their forefathers.[5]

Some of the points Meany presented with such admirable economy of expression in 1901 now call for greater elaboration if we are to understand both the full ramifications of his statements and the context in which he made them. The following glosses and notes should suffice:

1. Mining on the "South Half." The lure of gold was catching; even Barnett Stillwell, the Indian agency teacher, was involved in amateur prospecting and Henry Steele was shortly to devote some of his time to assaying the gold brought into Steveson's store in Nespelem.

2. Indian farming and logging. It was Bureau of Indian Affairs policy to encourage Indians to exploit the natural resources of the reservations so that the reservations would become self-supporting, thus requiring less expenditure of funds raised by taxes on the general American public; the Indians would thereby pay for the Bureau that had been appointed to govern them. "They mark their own logs": in traditional Plateau culture the land and its products were in the collective stewardship of the tribe as a whole, but in the reservation era every effort was made to get Indians to respect individual ownership of property. The acquisition of property was viewed as one of the most effective methods of Americanization.

3. The school, as we shall see, was another Americanizer.

4. Liquor. Whisky trafficking onto a reservation as large as the Colville was hard to police, and there were occasional charges in the press to the effect that even agency employees were involved in it. While none of the whites at Nespelem was ever accused, at least one of them, and possibly two, had problems with drink. One of the most notorious Indian whisky traders was a ruthless outlaw Okanogan named Puckmiakin. He would trade horses for whisky from whites and whisky for horses from Indians. He was known to have murdered at least three men with his own hands and his whisky certainly fired one man, Yayoskin, a nephew of Chief Moses, into a drunken frenzy during which he beat his own brother's brains out. Puckmiakin himself was murdered in 1893, but the trafficking continued. Alcohol was worse than a plague to the Indians. To people who in one generation had had to suffer a complete change of life style from that of free roaming, hunting, fishing, and vegetable-growing to one of enforced idleness around the doors of the agency—or, at best, a life of inadequate farming—whisky provided a temporary pleasure, a relief from that sense of waste, then oblivion.

5. Indian Inspector James McLaughlin. Meany submitted his thesis, and received his degree, in the late summer of 1901, before the matter of Joseph's homeland had been settled. But his thesis was right in stressing that McLaughlin's dispatches had been against Joseph's position. McLaughlin was not totally unsympathetic to the chief. "Chief Joseph was most amiable and a very pleasant traveling companion throughout our trip to Wallowa Valley and return to the Colville reservation," he said. "He is quite intelligent and exceedingly shrewd. . . ."[6] McLaughlin's main objections were based on his conviction that Joseph's influence prevented other Nez Perces from expressing themselves. He believed that an insufficient majority really wanted to move—and on this question he was supplied with figures, admittedly incomplete, by Steele; that the land at Nespelem was better than available land at Wallowa, assuming the government could afford the high price which would be charged for it; and that the whites at Wallowa were opposed to Joseph's resettlement.

It should be remembered that to the Sioux people McLaughlin was known as White Hair. White Hair was the man who, in the period of alleged unrest during the rise of the Ghost Dance cult ten years earlier, had ordered the arrest of Sitting Bull. When the Indian policemen came to take him, both Sitting Bull and his son were murdered, and these events contributed to the tension leading to the infamous massacre of Big Foot's band at Wounded Knee. Also, in the story of his involvement with Joseph that McLaughlin recorded in *My Friend the Indian* (1910), Joseph was shown as less attractive than he appeared in McLaughlin's own earlier reports, thus "justifying" further the decision made against the chief. (Later, it was the aging Indian Inspector's name and authority that sealed the McLaughlin Agreement whereby the "South Half" of the Colville Reservation was thrown open to whites.)

It seems to have been the case that quite early on in his research for his thesis Meany conceived the idea of wedding his historical efforts and his concern

25. *Chief Joseph in Seattle, 1903* (Curtis).

26. *Colonel Enoch Pratt and General Howard with Chief Joseph, Carlisle Indian Industrial School, Pennsylvania, 1904* (photographer unknown). *Colonel Pratt was the commandant of the school for many years.*

27. *Start of the Fourth of July parade, Nespelem, 1900s* (Latham).
*Altogether some two hundred riders participated in these parades during the early years
of the century; this is part of the women's division. Joseph would start the
proceedings and preside over them.*

28. *Edmond S. Meany orating at the reburial of Chief Joseph, 1905* (Curtis).

29. *Chief Yellow Bull, 1905* (Latham). *Yellow Bull was blind and aged when he posed for this picture at the time of the reburial ceremonies. He wore a red robe trimmed with ermine. Since he rode the dead chief's favorite horse and wore his eagle headdress to deliver one of his speeches, the headdress shown here may once have belonged to Joseph himself.*

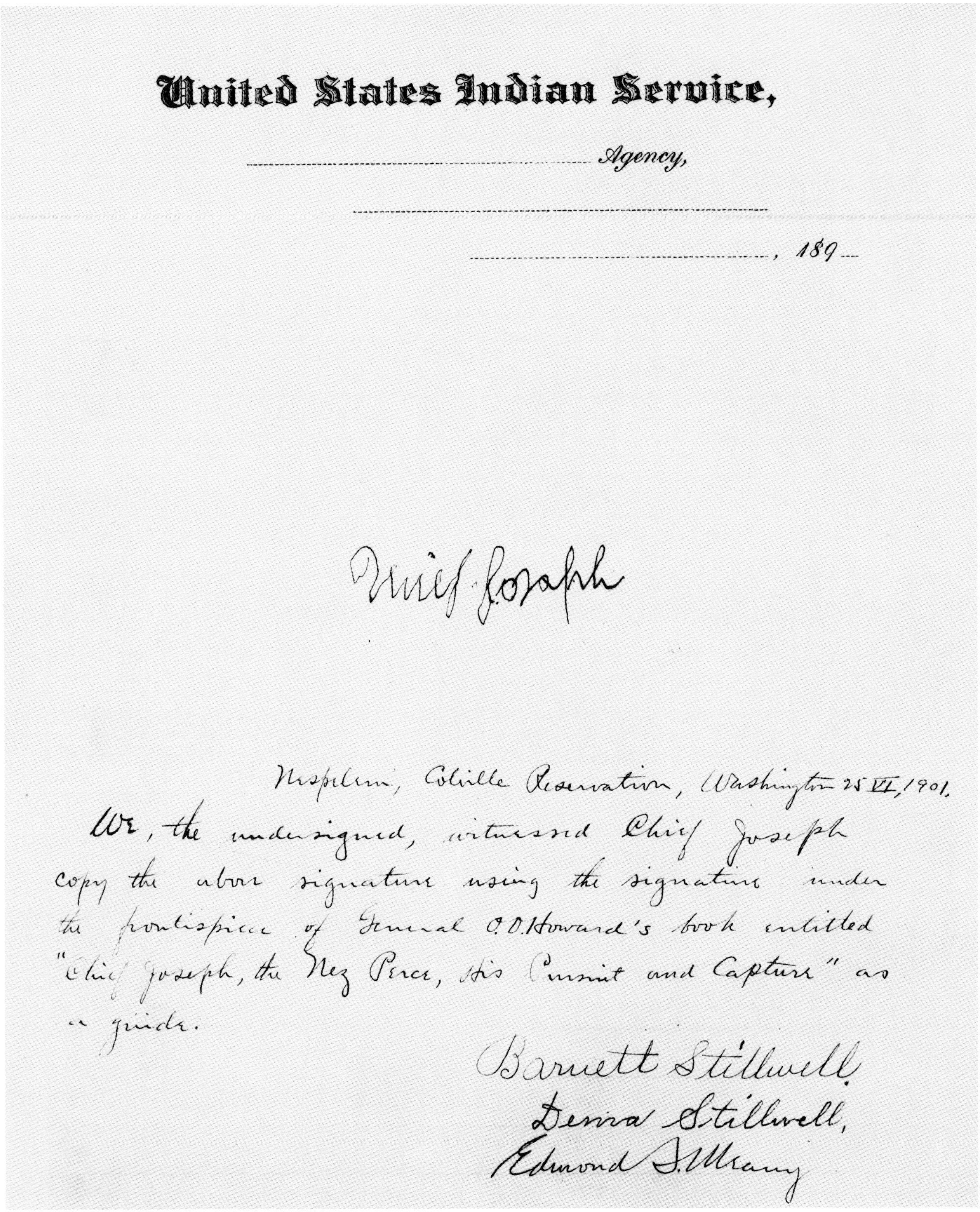

United States Indian Service,

--- Agency,

--- , 189 ---

Chief Joseph

Nespilem, Colville Reservation, Washington 25 VI, 1901.

We, the undersigned, witnessed Chief Joseph copy the above signature using the signature under the frontispiece of General O.O. Howard's book entitled "Chief Joseph, the Nez Perce, His Pursuit and Capture" as a guide.

Barnett Stillwell,
Denna Stillwell,
Edmond S. Meany

30. *Chief Joseph's signature, 1901* (procured by Edmond S. Meany).

31. *Chief Joseph's tepees, summer 1901* (Meany).

32. *Chief Joseph's winter quarters, c. 1901* (Latham). *The composite tepee on the left was a type much favored by Plateau people for large gatherings.*

33. *Chief Joseph's winter quarters, c. 1901* (Latham). *In this view of the quarters the mixture of traditional reed mats and modern canvas in the construction of the tepee is apparent.*

34. *Chief Joseph's abandoned house, summer 1901* (Meany). *Meany reported that "the Chief will not live in his house and the roof of his barn is broken in."*

35. *Chief Joseph's abandoned barn, summer 1901* (Meany).

36. *Luke Wolfhead's home, c. 1901* (Latham). *On the back of his own print of this photograph, Meany wrote, "only house built by a Nez Perce at Nespelem."*

37. *The saw and grist mill at Nespelem, c. 1901 (Latham). According to Steele, "Mr. Anderson has . . . refused them any benefits from the sawmill or blacksmith shop."*

38. *Ada and Emma Stillwell with Nez Perce children, c. 1901 (Latham). In 1903 Barnett Stillwell wrote to Professor Meany about Ada: "your little interpreter thinks [you] ought to know she is willing to act as interpreter for Joseph."*

39. *Chief Joseph, July Fourth celebrations, Nespelem, 1900s (Latham). On the back of one print of this photograph a contemporary historian wrote, "before the Chief would pose for this picture . . . he extracted $10 from the artist." Dr. Latham himself said much the same in a newspaper item published on Christmas day, 1904, so it is conceivable that this is the photograph Latham was referring to when he wrote to Meany in July 1901: "I got two negatives of Joseph . . . but the old rascal fixed himself in a horrible shape, no one would know that it was Joseph, he painted himself . . . dead black, was covered all with white Eagle feathers. . . ."*

40. *Chief Joseph, 1903* (Curtis). *"Mr. Curtis makes a specialty of Indian heads, and he refused to take a full-length portrait of the old warrior. He took one picture of the chief wearing the elaborate headdress, and then he had Joseph take off his feathers for a picture of the plain head. . ."* [*P-I reporter*].

with present conditions by producing a full scale biography of his subject. While still gathering documents for his thesis he informed Commissioner of Indian Affairs Wesley A. Jones of his proposed life of the Nez Perce leader. It was the biography that insured his continuing entanglement with affairs at Nespelem, some two hundred miles from his bustling life in Seattle. For the Nez Perces this was a period of crisis. It was, perhaps, inevitable, considering McLaughlin's findings, that further moves would be initiated against their traditional ways, as the following correspondence shows.

Department of the Interior,
U.S. Indian Service

Nespelem, Wash. July 16" 1901

My Dear Professor:

I have been in receipt of your letter under date of the 28" ultimo, and you will please Kindly pardon me for my laxity and tardiness. I assure you, my time has been taken up since the 1st inst with the celebration here, which I am pleased to state, is on the wane.

I also take pleasure in acknowledging the receipt of the fish-pole, which reached me without mishap in transit. I cannot express my thanks for your kind consideration and thoughtfulness. While not an expert angler, I shall remember you while endeavoring to allure the wary trout. . . . I am now busy arranging details for the taking of Census and apprehend that this will take me fully a month. Dr. Latham secured some very fine negatives of Chief Joseph on the 4th and states that he will mail you a "sett" at an early date. The Dr is now at the Agency and I cannot state when he will return but I presume, shortly. Mr. Anderson has not arrived here as yet and we do not expect him until the 1st Proximo. We have broken up housekeeping and at present I am dining with Mr. Stillwell. A communication from the Hon Com. of Indian Affairs, states that the school here will hereafter be discontinued. We all deeply regret this for many reasons. Any information you may wish in compiling your work, that I may be able to furnish, do not be timid to write me and I shall gladly furnish it. I hope your visit to the capital city, of my native state [Wisconsin] will be both pleasant and profitable. I shall be pleased to hear from you and with many warm personal regards

Believe me Sincerely
Henry M. Steele

Nespilem, Wn Aug. 18" 1901

My Dear Professor—

Yours of the 9" Inst has reached me and note what you say . . . Mr. Stillwell is now at Lakeside, Wash. and expects to remain there. I sincerely Congratulate you in securing the title of Master of Letters at Madison Wis. and hope it will add to your success in the literary and historical world. I am about to leave the Indian Service for reasons better known to myself. I assure you, to a certain extent, my exit is not regretted by myself and perhaps, a consolation and satisfaction to others. I will remain at Nespilem and expect to have a long interview with Chief Joseph after my suspension, which may eventually mean my removal. However, any assistance I may be able to render you, do not feel in any way timid in asking it. With many kind remembrances believe me

Very Truly
Henry M. Steele

Office of
Barnett Stillwell

Notary Public
Real Estate
Insurance

Chelan, Washington, Oct 17th 1901

Edmond S. Meany,

My Dear Professor—

Your welcome letter and the package of photos arrived safely some time ago. Many thanks for the photos. They took me back to the reservation again as I was familiar with every line in the pictures. I would be glad to send you some pictures of Mrs. S. and myself but we have none at present. . . .

Lake Chelan is a charming body of water and the climate too is everything it should be. The town is new. . . . This place is destined to be a great summer resort.

Your little interpreter [Stillwell's daughter] is going to school. She is growing like a bad weed. She created consternation among a group of Indian women here one day by addressing them in their own language.

When I entered the Indian Service [I] did not realize the value of the folklore stories you speak of. My tastes run that way very much, but my leisure time at Nespelem was all taken with mining and hunting. I used often to think that I would be doing the right thing by letting the mining go and devoting myself to folklore stories. . . . About the time I left Nespelem many miners were going there and there seems to be a rush to that locality. It is evident I left just the wrong time.

My business as real estate agent is not thriving as it should. About next spring will be in better shape. We have a nice little home and are enjoying life. I rejoice to say the people seem to be genuine good people. I think we will like it.

Mrs. S. and the little girls join me in sending the best of wishes. We should like to hear from you often.

Very truly your friend,
Barnett Stillwell

E. T. Steveson
Dealer in
General Merchandise and Miners' Supplies

Nespelim, Wash., Oct 28" 1901

My Dear Prof.

I have been in receipt of your letter under date of the 18" ultimo and I hope you will kindly pardon my extreme negligence. I have been busy arranging my new quarters and have just taken possession. I am also employed in Mr. Steveson's store, and taking all matters into consideration, I assure you my time has been taken up since I left the service. I have just interviewed Chief Joseph and in answer to your query, as to what tribe his mother was a member he says: "My mother was not a Cayuse, she was a full blooded Nez Perce and her name was E-tow-een-my. My mother's father's name was Kol-la-poon, and he was also a full blooded Nez Perce."

Chief Joseph is reluctant about giving any information about his children. They are all dead and from what I can understand they dislike to discuss the memories of the departed. He states however, if you should come here he would tell you all about them, how many, their names, where they died etc. The chief has been sick for the past week but is able to be out and around. He is now having considerable trouble with his Agent, Mr. Anderson. Mr. Anderson it seems requested Joseph to send the children of his tribe to Ft. Spokane Boarding School. This he refuses to do, claiming that a treaty some time ago, gave them a school here at Nespilem. Mr. Anderson has discontinued issuing them rations and also refused them any benefits from the saw mill or blacksmith shop. In fact at the present time, Joseph and his small band are enjoying no assistance from the gov't whatever. Joseph starts for Spokane tomorrow to get legal advice in the matter and also communicate with the authorities at Washington. Since leaving the service, I have refrained from expressing my opinion on affairs of this kind wither pro or con and shall follow this course while I reside here. It seems to me that Joseph has good reasons to complain. It is difficult to predict the outcome but at present the outlook surely portends no benefit. . . . I am now a full fledged Notary Public. This with my Recording work, keeps me rather busy. I am pleased to state that I am doing as well, if not better than while on the Indian service besides being extricated from all the entanglements of petty politics.

I shall be pleased to furnish from time to time any data you desire in reference to Joseph's life, that is, any thing I can get. The Chief and myself are on very friendly terms and he furnishes me with information denied to others.

I presume you are busy with College matters and apprehend your duties are many. About what date do you expect your work on Joseph's life to be completed? With warm personal regards and kind remembrances.

Believe me Sincerely
Henry M. Steele

Department of the Interior,
U.S. Indian Service.

Colville Agency,—Miles, Wash.
November 6, 1901

Prof. Edmund [sic] S. Meany,
State University,
Seattle, Washington.

My dear Meany:—

I have received your letter from Spokane dated the 2nd instant and was glad to hear from you. Wonder why I did not hear from you from Madison. I wrote you twice but failed to get an answer.

Yes, Joseph is somewhat disappointed, but the old rascal does not seem willing to do the right thing in any matter and is now strenuously opposing sending the children of his tribe to school. I have had to retaliate, or rather punish him, for his obstinancy by shutting off all issues to his people and that, I think, will bring him to time shortly. I am perfectly willing that he should go to Washington. In fact, I am anxious to have him go, for I am certain that he will get the proper reception when he gets there, as the Department is not only aware of the course I am pursuing, but heartily approve of my action.

I shall be in Seattle within a few days, possibly before the end of this week, when I will call and hope to find you at home.

Very sincerely,
A. M. Anderson

Department of the Interior,
U.S. Indian Service

Nespilem, January 20, 1902

Prof Meany.

Dear Sir: I received your letter by last mail. All of the portraits I sent you are Nez Perce. To secure the portrait of Joseph's two Squaws would be almost as impossible as to solve the problem of perpetual motion. A Nez Perce has no use for a woman only as a beast of burden and to sleep with, they are looked upon as an inferior being and are not as well cared for as his horse. As grasping and selfish as old Joseph is, I do not think any inducement could be brought to bear to have his portrait taken with his women. Old Chief Moses was just the opposite, he was always proud of Mary and on all occasions would tell what a good woman she was, he never went any place without her and she always drove the horses and took care of the money. Joseph and his people are very ugly this winter. The day school here was done away with[.] the Gov't made a strong effort to have the children sent to the Fort Spokane School. the Columbias consented but Joseph positively refused, so his rations were stopped and he and his people get no benefit of the Mill or Blacksmith shop. They are ugly and surly[.] I do not see Joseph oftener than once or twice a month. If you could come here in the Spring I will try to get you any pictures you might wish. I would want to wait until after the leaves came out so as to get a good back ground and besides the light would be much stronger.

I presume you know that Steele is out of the service[.] he went to Spokane about three weeks since and has not returned

Very truly
Dr. E. H. Latham

It is clear that the main hostility toward Joseph and his people during the crisis emanated from Agent Anderson himself. He hated Joseph precisely to the degree that the chief represented *Indianness;* indeed, to Anderson, as to so many policy makers and administrators in the Indian Service, the very word "Indian" was sometimes used as a term of opprobrium. When the Bureau's efforts were being channelled into pressing Native Americans into "citizens' dress," a man like Joseph could easily come to be thought of as a counterforce. He was described in this way in Anderson's contribution to the *Annual Report* for 1899:

Chief Joseph himself is not in any way a progressive Indian. . . . It is difficult to instill in his mind the fundamental principles of civilization. He lacks the stamina of a chief. . . . [He] may be applauded for . . . acts of bravery. . . . All these acts appear very flattering on the pages of history, but to know a man thoroughly is to see him daily, [and] as a progressive, public spirited Indian he is decidedly a sad failure. . . . He should be willing to elevate his people to a higher standard . . . [but] they plod along in the same rut from year to year.[7]

The reason the Nez Perce leader opposed sending the tribe's children away to boarding school at Fort Spokane—located just outside the Colville Reservation across the Columbia near the Spokane Reservation—was that the children would be *totally* removed from traditional tribal influences. The speaking of aboriginal languages, even the Chinook Jargon, was forbidden on pain of punishment at the boarding schools. Hair was cropped. And, of course, pupils were habituated to white customs and beliefs. Fort Spokane was particularly alien; it had been an army barracks and something of a militaristic atmosphere continued to pervade it after the army vacated the premises. So the situation in 1901 was an uncomfortable one. When Joseph held to his resolve not to let the children travel to Fort Spokane and the Nez Perce rations were cut off, it became tense.

Steele sent his resignation to Anderson on August 21, 1901. The agency files show that in the worsening climate he was unable to sustain the neutral position he at least claimed to hold when he wrote to Meany in October. The

Nez Perces were hungry and bitter, while the white agency employees proved intransigent, even hostile. Steele recommended a Spokane lawyer to Chief Joseph and gave him a letter of introduction. The lawyer was probably R. B. Scott, himself part Indian. In the course of his meeting with the lawyer, Joseph asked him to look into the possibility of bringing about the outright dismissal of Anderson, Thomas McCrossen (who had issued, apparently, no rations since his appointment as Steele's successor), various other functionaries, and Latham (who, it was said, refused to visit the sick in their homes). Steele did not report all this to Professor Meany. The evidence is taken from McCrossen's letters to Anderson. He had joined the Indian service as a watchman and carpenter, so it was a big promotion when he took over from Steele as additional farmer and subagent. Perhaps this made him more zealous in the performance of his duties. In communications dated October 29 and November 4 he kept Anderson informed of the chief's movements. And it is clear from a long letter from McCrossen to Anderson of November 7 that Steele was also under observation; the letter relays an Indian informer's tales of a meeting between Joseph and his senior men to report on his visit to the lawyer in Spokane.

On this occasion neither the Nez Perces and Joseph, nor Steele, was successful. Joseph ultimately had to allow the children to attend school at Fort Spokane and the food rations were reinstated. But the experience probably gave renewed life to Joseph's desire to get away from Nespelem and back to the Wallowa Valley.

II

Joseph emphatically did not "lack the stamina of a chief." He traveled to Washington and sent pleas to white people he believed had influence. At that time Joseph was almost certainly the most famous of the surviving patriot chiefs, so his cause did attract attention and some aid. Among his supporters was Samuel Hill, the telephone, railroad, and property magnate. Hill was rich and already eccentric (though in his later years, when he became a homemaker and provider for deposed eastern European royalty, he grew much more so). He had married the daughter of James J. Hill, president of the Northern Pacific Railroad, and was building Maryhill for her, a concrete replica of a European stately home with a commanding view over the Columbia River. He collected Native American and other antiquities to decorate his home. And he saw himself as something of a patron towards certain Pacific Northwest men with artistic and literary aspirations, including Edward Curtis and Edmond Meany. Through the cooperation of Hill and Meany—Hill provided the money and Meany did the organizing—Chief Joseph was invited to deliver addresses in Seattle.

In unsigned articles for both the *Seattle Times* and the *Post-Intelligencer* on November 15, 1903, Meany announced Joseph's visit in terms meant to whip up public interest, and his piece in the *Post-Intelligencer* was accompanied by an extremely handsome photographic portrait of Joseph that had been done during one of the chief's visits to Washington, D.C. As a result of the publicity, Meany heard from Barnett Stillwell, who offered his daughter's services as interpreter, a task she had successfully undertaken for Meany during his 1901 visit to Nespelem: "your little interpreter," Stillwell wrote on November 16, "thinks you'd ought to know she is willing to act as interpreter for Joseph in this case." As it turned out, Henry Steele was to hold that position.

When it was known that Joseph—accompanied by Red Thunder, his nephew—was coming to Seattle, Frank La Roche, who had made his name by taking fine photographs of prospectors and "actresses" on the way to the Klondike in the nineties, asked Meany if he could make portraits of the chiefs: "If you will bring them to my studio," he wrote, "I will make a large photo head of each of them and present the [University of Washington State Historical] society with a copie of each. In Indian costume preferred."[8] La Roche, who had taken quite a few Indian pictures, was by no means the only photographer interested in Joseph. Out on the reservation Dr. Latham spent much of his spare time making likenesses of the Indians. Earlier, in 1901, he had given Meany an account of his efforts to portray Joseph:

I got two negatives of Joseph, these I developed and they are good, but the old rascal fixed himself in a horrible shape, no one would know that it was Joseph, he painted himself, or his face dead black, was covered all with white Eagle feathers, was riding a poor old bony horse that he had, whitewashed to a dead white, the old scoundrel made me pay him ten dollars in advance, had I known how he was going to fix himself I would not have given him anything. I have some four or five dozen plates exposed which I will try to develop before I go [*photographing in*] *the mountains.*[9]

On Christmas day 1901 Latham despatched to Meany a whole group of his photographs. On October 29 of the following year he sent Meany a photograph of Joseph that he had procured the previous winter. On November 12, 1902, he agreed to let Meany use Joseph's picture in his work "or in the paper," saying, "all I ask is that the copywright notice accompanies it," and he offered Meany's friends Indian pictures for "$4.00 per dozen unmounted or $5.00 mounted."

But, it seems to me, the honor of making the most lasting and profoundly penetrating portraits of Joseph at this period went to Curtis. In 1903, although he was not yet being heavily subsidized by J. Pierpont Morgan, Curtis had already formed his basic conception of what was to become his massive multivolume work, *The North American Indian* (1907–30), and was spending what time he could away from his Seattle studio collecting pictures and data in the field. The experience and insight he was to bring to bear in presenting Red Cloud, for instance, or Geronimo, or Plenty Coups, he brought to his 1903 studio portraits of Joseph.

For his part, Joseph seems to have evoked a mixed response in Seattle. The

Times of November 20 carried a straight report of his ultimate objective in coming to Seattle: the return to the Nez Perce people of the land in Oregon. The following day the same newspaper gave a full account of his speech at the Seattle theater: after opening remarks by Judge C. H. Hanford, Edmond Meany spoke of the chief's exploits and "especially when some glowing reference was made to him, [Joseph] would look pleased for a moment";[10] Joseph's own short speech, delivered in all his finery and translated by Steele, was well received by the audience. Meany had taken Chief Joseph to a football game, and the chief's understandable bemusement was duly reported by the *Times*. The reporter for the *Post-Intelligencer*, by contrast, filed a story full of ironies. The opening of this—under headings of JOSEPH HAS A HARD DAY; *Nez Perces Chief Sees First Football*; SMILES THREE TIMES; *Two Short Words Are Enough for an Entire Afternoon's Conversation*; SAVING HIMSELF FOR SPEECH—ran as follows:

Chief Joseph, the last of the Nez Perces, spent a strenuous day in Seattle yesterday. It was his first visit to the metropolis of the Northwest, and he made the most of his time. With his friend Prof. Edmond S. Meany, whom he has nicknamed "Three Knives," and his nephew, Red Thunder, the old chief went out to Athletic park yesterday afternoon and saw his first football game. Last night he told a lot of people in the Seattle theater that the agents of the government were great liars, and that he wanted to go home to the Wallowa country to die.

The old chief is beginning to feel his age, and when he had stood in the mud and slush on the sidelines at the football game for a couple of hours he began to feel the rheumatism in his knees, and then his friend Three Knives picked out the wrong car to get home on, so that the old man had to climb the Madison Street hill to reach the Lincoln hotel. He arrived, barely able to walk, wheezing like a locomotive and able to mutter but one word, "Tired!" "Tired!"[11]

It may be that the *Post-Intelligencer's* anonymous reporter had a grudge against Meany that he was keen to work off in his story; he recorded that Joseph and Red Thunder spent a quiet morning in their hotel room "but at 1 o'clock in the afternoon the tall form of Three Knives came swinging in between the glass doors." "Their troubles," he added, "began right there." And throughout most of the long article Meany was presented as an accident-prone buffoon. It is also possible that the unknown author was characteristically misanthropic, the kind of writer who delights in regaling the public with the weaknesses of other humans (especially those with a claim to fame), whoever they may be. As a consequence, the football game at the university, some four miles from the chief's hotel—with its rooters' chorus, its displays of sporting viciousness, its power to bring Meany to a state of childish excitement and involvement, its general mass hysteria—were all presented with as detached an eye as Joseph must have seen them with. Similarly, the alienness of the Indians—Joseph "bowlegged and broadchested, . . . his small feet enclosed . . . in nice new boots

. . . [and] on his head . . . one of those wide cowboy hats that Frederic Remington puts on his characters . . . [with] a red handkerchief, knotted, . . . around his neck"—was depicted with a sharp precision that is especially noticeable in the account of what the writer referred to as the chief's second smile of the afternoon:

He smiled again when a bit of a boy, wearing a bright red sweater and a look of assurance, swaggered up to the old man and extended a dirty paw for a hand shake. The old Indian poked out a little finger for the lad to shake. The boy thought this the Indian style of handshaking, and he, too, stuck out his little finger, and they touched fingers. That was smile No. 2.

The report also has a scent of animus against Joseph or against Native Americans in general; at least, it is difficult to explain its author's deliberate lack of sensitivity in any other way. The awe and fear of the two Indians when confronted by the hotel's unfamiliar elevator, for example, or their bemusement at the invisible power motivating the streetcar, or Joseph's dress eagle hat "that flapped as he walked, like the feathers on the hats of the Florodora girls," were all exhibited with positive glee. But the antagonism, if such it was, is most apparent in the description of Joseph's speech itself:

He took a long drink of water, and then leaned one hand heavily on a table. Henry Steele, who came over with him, stood alongside him to act as interpreter. Then when the people in the audience were all keyed up to listen to the wonderful orator, the stories of whose eloquence have been thundering down the corridors of time for the past twenty years, the old man found his voice and began to speak.

"Um-mum-mum-halo-tum-tum-um-mum" was the way it sounded to the audience.

"Today my heart is far away from here," Mr. Steele said Joseph said.

"Um-mum-cumtux-alcamoose-ta-ra-ra!" exclaimed the old warrior, warming a little to his work.

"I would like to be back in my old home in the Wallowa country; my father and children are buried there, and I want to go back there to die," was what the chief really said, according to Mr. Steele.

"Hi-yu, mum-um-tum-tum," mumbled Joseph, laying one hand on his heart and rolling his eyes upward.

"The white father promised me long ago that I could go back to my home, but the white men are big liars," interpreted Mr. Steele, and then the white men in the audience laughed.

And That Was All

"Kopet," grunted the old chief, sitting down with a thud.
"That's all," said Mr. Steele, and then the people looked at each other and

began to smile. What about his record as a soldier, and what of all the inside history of that wonderful running fight he was to tell about? Joseph did not have a word to say about that; all he is interested in is getting back to his old home.

But if Chief Joseph did not care to dwell upon his record as a soldier and as a leader of men, his friend Three Knives was there to tell about it, and he told it well. Joseph may be a wonderful strategist, strong and resourceful in battle, but as an orator his friend Three Knives has him looking like a man who never was.

The anonymous reporter ended his account with the information that Joseph would be having his picture taken by Curtis during his stay in the city. Sure enough, Joseph did meet Curtis the following day, Sunday, and was photographed. The *Post-Intelligencer* reporter managed to excel even himself in the weight of sarcasm and innuendo he shovelled into his new story:

OLD CHIEF LIKES CITY
Joseph Meets a Famous Indian Artist
THEN TAKES A BATH
Enjoys His Swim and Grunts His Approval of White Man's Conveniences
VISIT UNIVERSITY TOMORROW

Chief Joseph got up from a nice, soft bed in the Lincoln hotel yesterday morning just as the fog was lifting off the bay, and grunting a good morning to Red Thunder, the two chiefs stood at the window watching the ships come in. The old chief's joints were still stiff from his experience out on the football field, and he walked like a man who is treading on eggs.

He was in high good humor with himself, however, for women had crowded around him after his great speech in the Seattle opera house and begged him for his autograph. Now Joseph has contended all along that he cannot write his name, except to trace it after Mr. Steele has written it. It took a lot of coaxing to get the chief to sign the article giving the Post-Intelligencer *his opinion of the great American game of football, and he refused absolutely to touch pen to paper until Mr. Steele had written the name; then Joseph traced the letters slowly in a trembling hand.*

But when the women crowded around him, patted him on the back and told him what a wonderful man he was, the old chief thawed out wonderfully, and he scrawled his name on bits of paper for them. The burden of Joseph's cry has been these last few years that all white men are liars because they promise to send him home, and they don't do it. His actions regarding his ability to write are conclusive evidence that Joseph has absorbed some of the traits of the white man at least.

After a hearty breakfast Chief Joseph and Red Thunder sat around the hotel waiting for Three Knives to come in with his sunny smile. Mr. Steel [sic] was sick all day yesterday and remained in bed most of the day, so Three Knives acted as escort to the Indians down to Curtis' studio to have their pictures taken.

The old chief still shies at elevators and he backed into the elevator that took him up to the studio. Once inside it seemed to him that he had butted right in on a big Indian council, for the faces of Indians of a dozen different tribes looked at him from the walls. The old man got a little suspicious, and he would not sit down until he had felt all the walls and looked around, planning a way of retreat in case a hasty flight became necessary.

Mr. Curtis is a professional Indian tamer, his long experience among them enabling him to take a refractory savage and slow him down until he is tame enough to feed from the hand, so he and Joseph became tillicums right away. Mr. Curtis knew things about the Nez Perces that Joseph had never heard of, and then he could tell stories about Indians that Joseph did not know were on earth. If Joseph came to Seattle thinking he was the only chief in the world, he knows better now, for yesterday he saw the pictures of a dozen chiefs of as many different tribes.

Joseph was much interested in the collection of Mojave Indian heads that Mr. Curtis got last summer while in the Southwest, and he wanted to know all about the Indian girls whose pictures he saw. The old man is something of a prude, for he told Mr. Curtis in unmistakable sign language that he did not approve of girls having their pictures taken with bare shoulders. The old gentleman sees nothing wrong, however, in having two wives.

Strange as it may seem, Mr. Curtis and Chief Joseph had never met until yesterday. Mr. Curtis knows a number of friends of Joseph, but had never encountered the old chief before. The old chief was quite eager to have his picture taken, and went about making that elaborate toilet that kept the audience in the Seattle theater Friday night waiting so long. He finally came out of the dressing room, looking like a turkey cock on dress parade, and, shoving one foot to the front and resting the other so heavily that it bowed his leg, signified that he was ready for hostilities to begin.

Mr. Curtis makes a specialty of Indian heads, and he refused to take a full-length portrait of the old warrior. He took one picture of the chief while wearing the elaborate headdress, and then he had Joseph take off his feathers for a picture of the plain head.

"Had I been able to get a picture of Chief Joseph as he sat on the stage of the Seattle theater last night, with his head on his breast and his eyes closed, listening to the eloquent address of Prof. Meany, it would have been a better study than anything I got today," said Mr. Curtis.

"I do not consider that Chief Joseph's head is a good type of the Indian, nor is he the best to be found among the Nez Perces. True, he is getting old, and his face is somewhat puffy, but allowing for that, there are much finer types to be found among his own people right now. Had I been able to catch him as he was last night, unconscious of his sourroundings [sic] and thinking only of his wrongs, I would have had a study worth keeping, but today he knew that he was having his picture taken, and the effect is not so good."

Red Thunder wanted his picture taken also, and he donned his brass ornaments, feathers and buckskins. Mr. Curtis took a couple of heads for his own use, and then made a couple of pictures for the young chief. These must be full length, and Red Thunder posed himself holding a bow and arrow that he had picked up in the studio.

Three Knives had to go to Arlington to deliver a lecture last night, so he hurried his red friends back to the hotel.

"Believe I take a swim," said Three Knives, slapping his chest and starting for the bath room.

A sound of splashing came to Joseph as he sat in his stocking feet, wondering how much longer it would be before he could "go home to Wallowa," and pretty soon Three Knives came out, looking fresh as a bud after an April shower, and announcing that he "felt fine."

"You swim?" asked the old chief, surveying Prof. Meany.

"Sure, me swim," replied Three Knives, slapping himself again.

"See, here is the water," and the professor dabbled his hands in the porcelain tub. The old chief felt the warm water running out of the faucet for a moment, and then paralayzed [sic] Three Knives with the announcement:

"Me swim, too," and straightway began a disrobing act. Three Knives fled into the next room, and soon there came a sound of a mighty splashing, as the boss of all the Nez Perces disported himself in his bath.

A grunt was the only response to the question as to how he liked taking a swim in the house, and the old man spent a lot of time arranging his hair in just the right curls. Then he spread himself flat on his back on a lounge, and proceeded to take life easy the rest of the afternoon.

With Three Knives out of the city and Mr. Steele unable to be with them on account of sickness the two Indians put in a lonesome afternoon. Joseph grunted a couple of times at Red Thunder, the younger man did as much to his chief, and the conversation was closed for the day.

After dark, however, Red Thunder got to worrying about Mr. Steele, and he would not rest until a man had been sent up from downstairs with a key to unlock the room. When he found that Mr. Steele was all right, though still pretty sick, he grunted to signify that everything was all right, and then went into his own room to grunt to the chief that their white friend was slightly indisposed.

Red Thunder says that when at home on Sunday they always have services, and that Chief Joseph usually makes a little talk to his people. Mr. Steele says he has lived on the reservation fourteen years, and has never yet caught the Indians attending a religious service. Chief Joseph says all white men are liars, and since he has been here he has shown that he himself knows how to sidestep the truth when occasion demands it.

The two Indians do not know what the programme is for today. They are willing to do anything that will add to the enjoyment of their stay in the city, and are anxiously awaiting the return of Three Knives from Arlington, for he will know just what to do.

Tomorrow Prof. Meany will take Chief Joseph and Red Thunder out to the university, and when the undergraduates cut loose that siwash yell the old man will be sorry he ever surrendered to Col. Miles twenty-six years ago. The Indians will probably start for home tomorrow night. They are supposed to be still prisoners of war and not leave the reservation without permission of the agent, but Joseph comes and goes just about as he pleases.

He can do almost anything he pleases except "go home," and that is the thing he wants most to do. It is the burden of his song day in and out, and will be until he dies. "Home to the land of the winding waters," where his father lies buried, and where he wants to be laid away.[12]

It would not have been surprising if with but *one* witness like this anonymous reporter dogging his days Joseph had returned to his own valley, or even to his place of exile, immediately. But he stayed in the city for a further day and Meany recorded, almost formally, a declaration Joseph seems to have made to him at that time:

Chief Joseph extended his hands, palms down, and ran his forefingers together back and forth while looking into my eyes and said: "Nika tum tum pe mika tumtum kwak nesam cooley kahkwa; delate tilikums, mika pe nika." [My heart and your heart always run close together so; good friends, you and I.][13]

Joseph also addressed the weekly assembly of University of Washington students. Speaking to this assembly was considered an honor and the people invited to do so included such national figures as Jacob Riis, the reformer, and later, in 1912, when at the height of his fame, Edward S. Curtis.

III

When Henry Steele first arrived in Nespelem in 1893 he was keen to be up and doing, to get things moving, to make progress with the Indians. He could not understand, apparently, either the degree of cultural loss they had suffered or their consequent depression and apathy. He was brusque in his efforts to try to get them to build ferries (and one was wrecked by the Columbia in flood before it was even completed), to transport wood, to farm and to build fixed, frame houses. He was also quick tempered, not only with the Indians, but with other white employees such as sawyer Lew Wilmot, a crotchety veteran of the Nez Perce War, or the miller, J. S. Scribner. In a letter Latham wrote to his agent on March 10, 1894, he described how he and another employee had decided not to execute a plan to set up house across a creek for fear of offending Steele or causing "any hard feelings."[14]

During the years he had lived among the Indians, however, Steele seems to have mellowed, or, perhaps, to have become less sure of the rectitude of his position. From 1901 onwards he and Meany were developing a friendship by letter: he seemed self-effacing and, at times, almost torpid, though open-handed and sensitive, while Meany revealed himself as vain but generous and thrusting yet vulnerable. The following letter from Steele, mentioning Meany's reaction to a supposed insult in an earlier Steele letter, points up the nature of the man:

Office of   Mines and Mining . . .   Notary Public
Henry M. Steele   Dist. Recorder

                                              Nespelem Wash Dec 19" 1901

My Dear Professor—:

I am just in receipt of your letter date of the 14" Inst. I am indeed pleased to hear from and really do not know whether to take you seriously or not. In my former letter in which reference was made to your moccasins, I was perfectly honest in what I said, and the thought of commenting on the construction of your anatomy, was as foreign as the hereafter. As late as yesterday, I made inquiry of Mrs. Parsons who has the measure of your foot, if she had begun your moccasins, and she replied that she had not but, thought she could obtain some from her Indian friends, in a very short time. It has been my annual custom to send moccasins and gloves east to relatives during the Holidays but this year, I must forego this practice being unable to obtain what I wanted. It is true the Nez Perce Indians are making and selling gloves etc but their make is very inferior to those made by other Indians, especially the Nespilems. There are but few women here who can make buckskin near such as I wished to send you, and upon those I have been waiting. I hope in the near future, I will be able to forward your foot wear. I wish to say with all candor, frankness and my honor as a man, that no insinuation nor reflection was meant in my letter. . . . I am of very humble origin and occupy a very ordinary position in life, but have always been above that plane, wherein I had either the presumption or audacity to criticise the physical personality of my fellow man. In my estimation, "big feet" "long legs" or "red hair" or perhaps short legs, black hair and small feet, cut but a small figure, as to the brightness, intelligence and brains of any individual. The little "naked boy" in the picture, is a little girl the daughter of Yet-ta-eno-set. The latter is a Nez Perce but not a member of Joseph's band. . . . Chief Joseph is well and contemplates visiting the Capital City during the present winter. Wishing you the blessings of a very Merry Christmas and with warm personal regards.

                                              Believe me Sincerely
                                              Henry M. Steele

Meany and Steele frequently exchanged good wishes and gifts but, more important in the present context, Steele was keen to help Meany in his researches. He took down the story of Chica-ma-poo, or Old Jean, the oldest surviving Nez Perce at Nespelem, a woman who had fought like a male warrior during the 1877 war; he sent relevant clippings from the local papers; he urged Meany to press ahead of his rivals to be the "first in the field" with his Joseph biography; and he put Meany's questions to the aging chief, as is best illustrated by the following letter:

I had an interview with Chief Joseph and Red Thunder yesterday and succeeded in gaining the information you desired. Chief Joseph says that there was but one Capt John and that he was not killed at the skirmish between the volunteers and Nez Perce scouts. He says that "Old George" and "Capt John" were present at his surrender; that they were old men then, and have died and are both buried at Lapwai Idaho. I am quite positive that this information is authentic, coming as it does from such a reliable source. Joseph remembers both of the above parties well and beyond all possible doubt the accuracy of his version of the affair cannot be doubted, or contradicted.

I weighed Joseph today and he weighs precisely 197 pounds. He was not heavily [clothed?], which accounts for his being so light. If my memory serves me right, I weighed him about 5 years ago and he tipped the beams to 220. However he was heavily clad at that time, and I am inclined to think that he has failed in weight during the past 2 years. I also measured his height and he is just 5 ft 9 in, in moccasins. One would think from observation, that he is taller but the above is absolutely correct as I was careful to get the height exact.

Under separate cover I mail you proof of photograph taken by Dr. Latham of Chief Joseph's credentials, as member of Gen. Miles' staff, during his visit to N.Y. City in '98 [sic]. We could get a much better one I think by removing the glass, as the latter is broken. Perhaps it may be of service to you. The Dr. will mount some of those and when he does so, will mail you one or more as you wish.

Kindly advise me if Mr. [Samuel] Hill has returned yet. Chief Joseph will leave for Washington D.C. some time before or after the Holidays. I hope the very limited information I have given you, will be of service. . . .[15]

Steele was a natural intermediary—as he said, he had "frequently taken a few puffs [of the pipe] with [Joseph], especially during the Holidays, when good will and friendship is supposed to prevail among all"—and, in this role, he had accompanied Joseph's party on the visit to Seattle at the end of 1903.[16] On December 4, 1903, he wrote to report their safe return to Nespelem, saying: "Chief Joseph and Red Thunder have not completed their story of their trip to Seattle and they are still telling their friends of their very pleasant trip and kind treatment." But the journey also caused him work: he twice had to ask Meany to press Curtis to send the pictures of the Indians that had, apparently, been promised (Red Thunder seems to have been particularly insistent on this) and he labored hard to produce, with Joseph's help, the versions of what Joseph had said in his Seattle speeches.

It is appropriate that, for Meany at least, it was through Steele that the last news of Joseph came, less than a year after the chief had summoned what must have been his failing strength to speak in Seattle. On September 24, 1904, Meany received a postcard sent two days earlier: "Chief Joseph died last evening and was buried today. Hastily H. M. Steele."

A little later Steele wrote at length:

Nespilem, Wn 9/26" 04

My Dear Professor:—

Your telegram and letter have been received and I hope you will kindly pardon my [sic] for my negligence in not wiring you of Joseph's death. In fact, I was entirely taken up with the details of his burial, assisting in digging his grave, and assisting in carrying his body to its final resting place. I had charge of the whole affair, was at his side a few minutes after his death and really I cannot explain why I feel so, over the death of an Indian. I have lost a good dear friend who has often told me in the most endearing and pathetic language that he longed and sighed for his old home. I believe now that no white man enjoyed the confidence of Chief Joseph that I did. He portrayed to me in impassioned eloquence, his unhappy position, always hoping that when the end came, he would be in his old home and that he might rest by the side of his ancestors. But alas! the wish that he most dearly cherished was never realized. He died without a home, broken in spirit, but still retaining all the characteristics and customs of a lofty and elevated chieftain. I now think that he had a premonition of death, for he requested his wife on the day he died, to bring him his head-dress and other regalia saying: "I may die any time and wish to die as a chieftain." During her absence from their tent to secure the articles, he died and on her return found him lying in the tent, life having departed but a few minutes before.

I cannot say when his people will be back but think they will return soon. He will be exhumed at that time and a general funeral held. One of his wives is not here and on her return I presume the ceremonies will take place. I will find out their idea about his body being transferred to Wallowa vally and convey to you their wishes. I will also notify you of their return and what they intend to do. There are but 3 or 4 of his people here and I have wired them to come home immediately. I presume there will be the largest gathering of Indians at that time that we ever witnessed here. He did not receive the cigar case etc, that you sent him. It arrived the next day after his death. They showed it to me and Mrs. Joseph wished me to take it but I declined and stated that at some future time I may accept but not now. I have been delayed with telegrams, letters ect since his death and you will kindly pardon this letter if it is somewhat rambling as I have answered so many in the past 2 or 3 days. I assure you, that I will keep you posted on all proceedings later on, and especially in reference to his removal to Wallowa valley. With my kindest regards and expressing my whole-souled grief over the death of our friend

Sincerely yours
Henry M. Steele

41. *A Nez Perce man, 1899* (Curtis). *In 1903 Curtis is reputed to have said, "I do not consider that Chief Joseph's head is a good type of the Indian, nor is he the best to be found among the Nez Perces." He probably had something more like this studio portrait in mind; when he published it in* The North American Indian *it was captioned: "This portrait represents a splendid type of the Nez Perce man."*

42. *Nez Perce profile, 1910* (Curtis). *Again, presumably Curtis believed this likeness more "typical" than his view of Joseph.*

43. *Red Thunder, 1903* (Curtis). *"Red Thunder posed himself holding a bow and arrow that he had picked up in the studio." This illustration is made from a sepia postcard version of the portrait that Curtis produced in a series for commercial sale.*

44. *Nespelem beadwork, June 1905* (Latham). *"The Nez Perce Indians are making* [beadwork] *but their make is very inferior to those made by other Indians, especially the Nespilems"* [Steele].

45. *Chica-ma-poo, or Old Jean, c. 1903* (Latham). *Henry Steele enclosed a summary of Chica-ma-poo's life story, as she told it to him, in a letter to Meany of December 19, 1901. She recorded that she was ninety years old, "perhaps more," had been married twice, but only one of her nine children had survived. She remembered that she had deliberately joined the Nez Perce war effort in 1877, even against the wishes of her husband. She had vivid memories of burying the dead "among the rocks and in secret places" so that the army would not know their casualties. After the war she had escaped with White Bird and lived with the Sioux in Canada, though she eventually rejoined her people after their return from Indian Territory. The son who survived was also living at Nespelem. He was the great warrior, Yellow Wolf, the man whose life L. V. McWhorter recorded in* Yellow Wolf: His Own Story *(1940).*

46. *Chief Joseph, May 1903* (Latham). *This is the photograph about which Latham wrote to Meany, "I think it very shabby in the P. I. to publish my coppywrighted picture and not even give me any credit of any kind."*

47. *Portrait of Joseph, c. 1901* (Moorhouse). *As may be seen in the relevant detail of the next photograph, this is the portrait on which the relief of Joseph's head on the monument was based.*

48. *Monument to Chief Joseph, Nespelem, n.d.* (photographer unknown).

49. *Nez Perce camp, Nespelem, c. 1900* (Latham).

50. *Chief Joseph's last home (Curtis). This picture was made in 1905 during Curtis'*
attendance at the reburial and potlatch ceremonies.

51. *Nez Perce Indians digging Joseph's new grave, June 1905 (Meany). According to Meany, "Relays of Nez Perce young men dug the new grave large and deep." Since native practice was to dig graves shallow to allow the soul passage back and forth, the digging must have been done at the insistence of whites.*

Unveiling Monument Over Chief Joseph's Grave
At Nespelem Wash. June-20-1905 Maj. Moorhouse

52. *Unveiling the monument to Chief Joseph, June 20, 1905* (Moorhouse).

Unveiling Monument Over Chief Joseph's Grave"
At Nespelem Wash. June-20-1905 Maj. Moorhouse

53. *E. L. Farnsworth making the invocation* (Moorhouse).

He led his people
in the Nez Perce War
of 1877.
Died Sept. 21, 1904.
Aged
about 60 Years.

54. *Agent John McA. Webster with Nez Perce leaders at the monument* (Curtis).

55. *Yellow Bull speaks* (Curtis).

Unveiling Monument Over Chief Joseph's Grave"
At Nespelem Wash, June-20-1905 Maj. Moorhouse

56. *Albert Waters speaks* (Moorhouse). In the background on the left
Edward S. Curtis is kneeling to change a plate in his camera.

57. *Ess-ko-ess speaks* (Curtis).

58. *Professor Meany speaks* (Curtis). *"A college professor in a frock coat and silk hat did part of the talking"* [*Curtis*].

59. *Joseph's feast-of-the-dead lodge* (Curtis). *A composite tepee like this could hold an astonishing number of guests.*

60. *Yellow Bird, 1905* (Latham). *Yellow Bird was what Meany termed the "announcer" at the potlatch ceremonies and he was much concerned by Albert Waters' lack of leadership experience.*

61. *Yellow Bull speaks from horseback* (Curtis). *"This speech was made on horseback, while the old chief rode slowly three times around the outside of the big council lodge"* [*Meany*].

62. *David Williams, c. 1903* (Latham). *David Williams, who suffered an eye affliction, was, according to Meany, "a typical Nez Perce" and he "interpreted promptly and with force" so that the Salish-speaking Nespelems at the potlatch ceremony could understand what was going on among the Shahaptian-speaking Nez Perces.*

63. *A Nez Perce elder, June 1905* (Latham). *"During a rest in the dance an old warrior, suitably bedecked with furs and feathers and carrying in his hand a calumet, gave an oration in the Nez Perce language"* [Meany].

64. *Black Eagle, 1905, a nephew of Chief Joseph and one of those who contended to succeed him as chief* (Curtis).

65. *Professor Meany with Chief Red Cloud and friends, summer 1907 (Meyer). This was taken while Meany was in the field collecting anthropological data for Curtis. In fact, the Indian on the far left was Curtis' chief assistant among the Plains peoples, A. B. Upshaw, a Crow. Red Cloud, legendary leader of much of the Sioux nation, victor of battles against the U.S. army in the 1860s, was already blind in 1907. He died in 1909. Fred Meyer, an amateur photographer, met Meany in the field and later sent him this picture.*

66. *Three Eagles, 1910* (Curtis). *Three Eagles was one of Curtis' principal Nez Perce informants. In the years after 1905 he was somewhat agitated that he had not received the pictures that the photographer had promised him.*

67. *Barnett and Ada Stillwell, summer 1901* (Meany). *In 1927 Stillwell wrote to Meany for old pictures of Meany's "little interpreter."*

68. *Chief Joseph in Washington, D.C., 1897* (Sawyer). *Steele, who believed Curtis'*
pictures revealed Joseph as "wretched," may have thought that a portrait like this was
"the real Joseph." Wells M. Sawyer was employed as a photographer by the Bureau of
American Ethnology on a regular basis during the late 1890s.

69. *Bas-relief of Joseph's head by Olin Warner, 1889. Commissioned by C. E. S. Wood, General Howard's aide in the Nez Perce War, a copy of this plaque was donated to the Chief Joseph Dam by Erskine Wood, schoolboy guest in Joseph's camp some sixty years earlier.*

70. *Peo-peo Tholekt, 1905* (Curtis). *Peo-peo Tholekt, or Bird Alighting, was always concerned to try to have Joseph's remains returned to the Wallowa Valley in Oregon.*

71. *Chief David Williams, c. 1920* (photographer unknown). *He believed that Joseph's body should remain where it was, on the little knoll in Nespelem.*

NOTARY PUBLIC. MINES AND MINING.

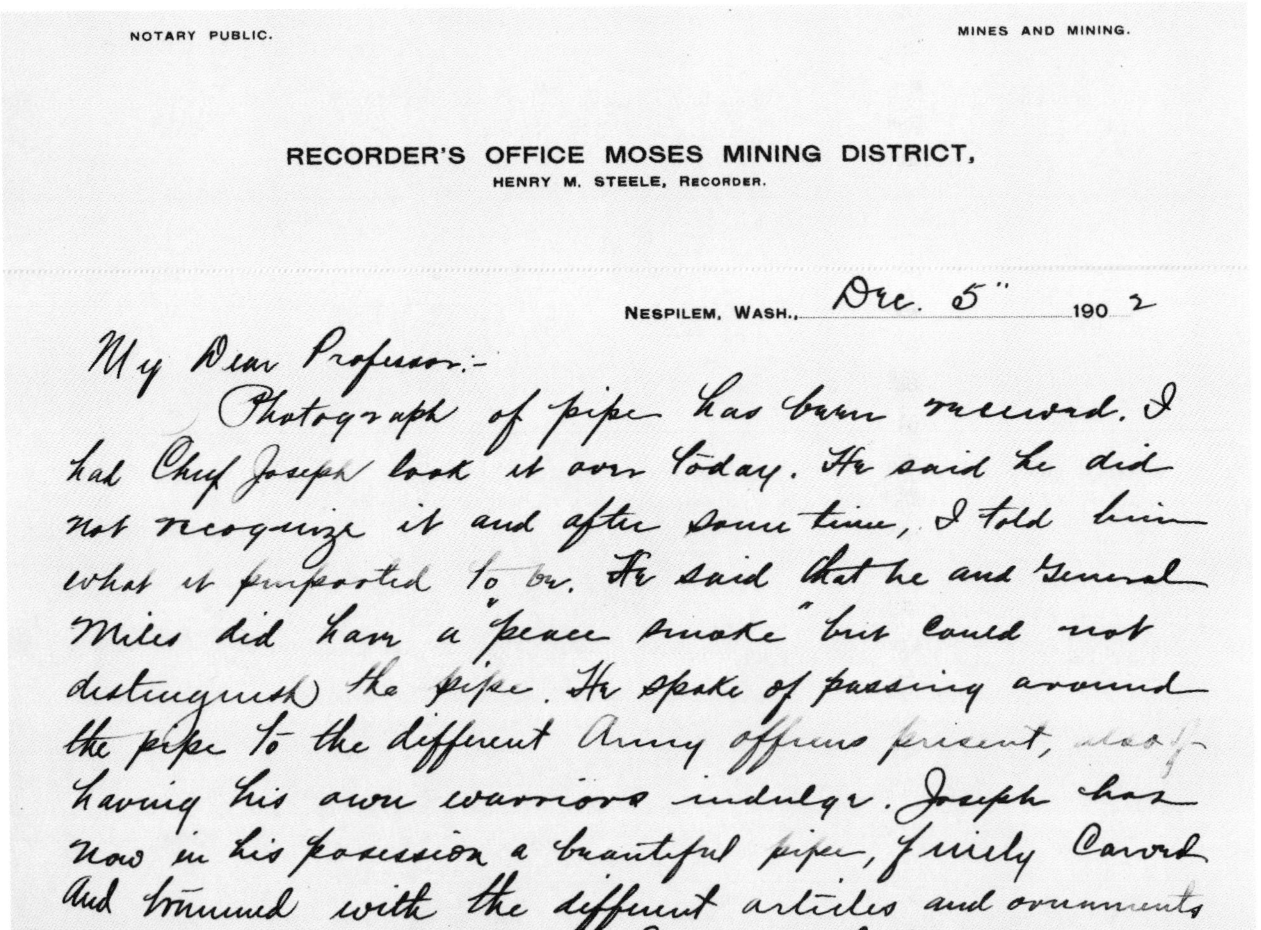

RECORDER'S OFFICE MOSES MINING DISTRICT,
HENRY M. STEELE, RECORDER.

NESPILEM, WASH., Dec. 5" 1902

My Dear Professor:-

Photograph of pipe has been received. I had Chief Joseph look it over today. He said he did not recognize it and after some time, I told him what it purported to be. He said that he and General Miles did have a "peace smoke" but could not distinguish the pipe. He spoke of passing around the pipe to the different Army officers present, also of having his own warriors indulge. Joseph has now in his possession a beautiful pipe, finely carved and trimmed with the different articles and ornaments originally used by the Indians. I have frequently taken a few puffs with him, especially during the Holidays, when good will and friendship is supposed to prevail among all. Joseph told me today that he thought of going to Washington soon. He has been to Spokane on a short visit and has just returned. Any further assistance I can render you, do not be timid in requesting it. With Kind regards

Very Truly
Henry M. Steele

Have received
No papers

72. *Letter of December 5, 1902 from Henry M. Steele to Professor Edmond S. Meany.*

Meany's immediate public response to the news of Joseph's death was an unsigned account for the *Seattle Times* entitled "College Students Mourn Death of Chief Joseph." In the course of this article, which was surmounted by a late photographic portrait of the chief and an example of his signature, Meany quoted from Steele's letter and broached his plans for the future:

Chief Joseph's death came with a sense of special loss to the University of Washington.

Many of the professors and students have expressed their feelings on the subject, and all of those who were there last year remember with peculiar interest the opportunity they had of hearing him and of shaking him by the hand. Professor Edmond S. Meany probably feels the loss most keenly as the chief and he had become close personal friends. The professor had visited Joseph at his home several years before the chief came to Seattle. Samuel Hill was responsible for Chief Joseph's visit to this city last year, and only a few weeks before the chief's death he visited him for the second time at the reservation. Seeing that Joseph was ill and desiring his autograph to be framed with his portrait he asked Professor Meany to arrange it. While arranging this matter the professor sent to the chief a present in exchange for the signatures, but the package arrived after his death.

Knowing that the chief's last wish, and in fact the principal hope of his life, was to die and be buried by the side of his father in the beautiful Wallowa Valley, the professor telegraphed his willingness to help carry out that last wish by transporting the body to its proper grave in that valley. The answer came from Henry M. Steele of Nespilem who for many years has been the closest of friends to Joseph.

This letter is full of pathos. The old chief had a premonition of death. He sent his wife from the tepee to the "ietas" house to get his robes of chieftainship telling her he might die at any moment. She hurried away, but on her return with his eagle hat and robes he was dead.

Joseph's people were away hop-picking at the time of his death and . . . Mr. Steele took charge of affairs temporarily when the chief died. He helped prepare the grave and also helped the few Indians present place the old hero in that temporary resting place. "I cannot explain," says he, "why I felt so over the death of an Indian. I have lost a good, dear friend who has often told me in the most endearing and pathetic language that he longed and sighed for his old home."

Professor Meany believes that if the Indians decide to carry the body of the old chief to Wallowa Valley there will be friends enough in Seattle and Spokane to help defray the expenses, and if it is decided to bury the body permanently at Nespilem, then these friends will probably unite and place above his grave a plain but rugged shaft of native granite to mark the last resting place of one of America's greatest Indians.[17]

The official account of Joseph's death, which appeared in the *Annual Report of the Commissioner of Indian Affairs*, was provided by Captain John McA. Webster, Agent Anderson having been removed from his post the previous May:

I sincerely regret to report that Joseph, chief of the Nez Perce, is dead at Nespelim, on the Colville Reservation. His death, resulting from heart failure, occurred at 5:45 P.M., September 21, and he was buried at noon on the following day. Most of his people were absent from Nespelim at the time on their annual pilgrimage to the hop fields around North Yakima, and the regular funeral services have been deferred until their return, which Mr. McCrossen, additional farmer at Nespelim sub-agency, writes me will be in a few days. Many of the Indians throughout this section are making arrangements to hold commemorative services at different points, showing the esteem in which he was generally held among them.

Chief Joseph has been ailing for some time past. Some six weeks ago he drove 75 miles over very rough roads to pay his respects to me here. At that time he looked thin, ill, broken in spirit, and complained of always feeling tired.

Joseph's death will probably have little appreciable effect on the future of his people. I find that he has been regarded as a malcontent, insubordinate, and not working for the best interests of his people. His long-continued refusal to consent to the education of the Nez Perce children caused him to be looked upon as nonprogressive and a stumbling block in the path of civilization. But I formed a different impression of the man. His demeanor was subordinate, meek, and pathetic. He declared that he had been utterly misunderstood and his motive misconstrued; that last year most of the available children of his tribe attended the school here, and that he would use his utmost endeavors to send in every one that could possibly be spared this year. He also indignantly disclaimed encouraging gambling and drunkenness among his people.[18]

Dr. Latham, as will be apparent, was not actually present when Joseph died, but his public response to the event was recorded in a newspaper interview:

CHIEF JOSEPH'S END DUE TO HIS GRIEF
BROKEN HEART SAID TO HAVE CAUSED DEATH

Thwarted Desire for Power and Longing for His Old Home at Wallowa Believed by His Physician to Have Broken His Spirit

WILBUR, Sept. 26.—(Special.)—"Chief Joseph died of a broken heart, follow-ing the conviction that in his old age he was unable to accomplish the desire *for power that had been nourished throughout a lifetime,"* said Dr. E. H. Latham, physician for the Indians at Nespelem, who for fourteen years was the medical advisor of Chief Joseph. Continuing, Dr. Latham said:

"Four years ago Joseph was attacked by a strange illness. I examined, studied him, and decided that grief was all that ailed him. In vain I tried to console him. His low spirits was followed by a real illness from pneumonia, but the magnificent physique of the man brought him through.

"From that time Joseph was never the same man. He brooded constantly over the fact that Wallowa, the country of his youth and of his dreams, was going farther and farther from him, and that the region about his new home at Nespelem was year by year growing smaller and smaller through the encroachment of the prospector and the settler. In recent months this grief has resulted in a bent form, in a listless life, which ended in death.

"The life of Joseph is worthy of emulation by many a white man. Although he was an Indian, Joseph was always a moral man, and always a temperate man. He was good to his squaws. He never separated from his first squaw, who is an old woman, and who was with him to the end. His other squaw, a woman in the forties, was ministering to him when he died. Although Joseph's Indian spirit prevented him from doing any work, he never abused either of these women. He often planned to lessen their burdens. Joseph abhorred intoxicating liquors, and always counseled his people to avoid liquor.

"With all of his sterling traits, Joseph was an Indian in many ways. He always harbored jealousy, and I am convinced that he never liked any white man. Admiration would be the better way of expressing his feeling for such friends as Gen. Miles. The funeral of Joseph will be a grand and ceremonious event, with an accompanying potlatch or feast and distribution of property. Above the grave of Joseph a bell will wave on a tall, slender pole of hemlock. Its tinkle will make peace with the spirits of the dead, according to an ancient Indian legend."[19]

It is worth noting that of this set of remarks the only one attributed by historians to Latham and repeated again and again—and which therefore characterizes the quality of his witness for most people—is his notion that Joseph died of a broken heart. As the full newspaper account above shows, Latham's feelings toward the chief were troublingly mixed. And it seems, like Joseph's toward him, they had been so for a long time. During his first two years on the reservation Latham had met with much resistance from Joseph to any white man's medicines, largely because of the miseries the Nez Perces had been subjected to in Indian Territory, but gradually Latham must have won him over. In 1893 Joseph had even joined Moses in requesting the authorities to transfer Latham back to the Nespelem Valley from Tonasket, a station in the Okanogan section of the reservation where he had been working for about a year. But Joseph's faith in white medicine could not have been anything like absolute; on March 1, 1894 Latham had confessed to his agent:

I am afraid my vaccinating scheme is going to be a failure. it seems that many of the Indians here were vaccinated in the Indian Territory and from some cause there were a great many deaths. Owhi says he came very near dying. They all seem to understand it and are as much afrade of vaccination as Smallpox. Moses says when warm weather comes if there is any danger of Small pox he will have his people submit, but I do not think the Nez Perces ever will. I have talked to them until I am talked out.[20]

On June 30, 1895, however, Latham had been able to report that during the winter he had nursed Joseph through a severe bout of pneumonia. At first he had refused to be treated but, at the urging of others, he had ultimately submitted. "It was a hard fight," wrote Latham, "but he recovered, and since then I have had no trouble with his tribe. if any are sick and they do not let me know he comes himself and goes with me to see that the medicine is taken according to directions."[21] Yet in 1900 there were rumors in the white press that Latham had failed to visit the quarantine area for five or six days during a smallpox epidemic and in 1901, as we have seen, Joseph seriously sought his dismissal.

It is thus not surprising that the doctor's personal reaction to Joseph's end was somewhat tangential to his public one. In a letter to Meany of October 4, 1904 he wrote: "I was not here at the time of Joseph's death and regret it very much indeed. he was buried before I returned, his people are all at Yakima gathering hops, upon their return they may have some doings but I do not think it will amount to much, if there is anything worth while I will try to get photoes." Then, with reference to one of the newspaper accounts of the chief's death, Latham added, "I think it very shabby in the P.I. to publish my coppywrighted picture and not even give me any credit of any kind."

Edmond Meany, for his part, was working hard at his teaching, at his administrative duties, and at the management of the University of Washington State Historical Society. In addition, he had just published an article on "Fox Farming in Alaska" in the August 1904 issue of Charles Lummis' magazine *Out West* and he distributed copies to parties he imagined would be interested (he sent a copy of virtually everything he wrote to the White House). Among those to respond to his gesture was Curtis (one of whose photographs for the Harriman Alaska Expedition of 1899 had been used as an illustration):

Dear Mr. Meany:—

Many thanks for the copy of "Out West". Well, our old friend chief Joseph has passed on. At last his long, endless fight for his return to the old home is at an end. For some strange reason, the thought of the old fellow's life and death gives me rather a feeling of sadness. Perhaps he was not quite what we in our minds had pictured him, but still I think he was one of the greatest men that has ever lived. I only wish that I could have had an opportunity to have spent more time with him and tried to learn more of his real nature. I believe that you should make the greatest effort possible to complete your work of his life and bring it before the publishers. Now should be as good a time as any.

My late trip to the Southwest has been a successful one. In no former trip have I accomplished so much in so short a time.

Most Sincerely,
E. S. Curtis

Seattle, Washington,
October thirteenth, Nineteen hundred and four

Meany's biography of the chief was, as it happened, virtually complete at the time of his death, or so he claimed. In a letter to Samuel Hill of September 9, 1904, less than two weeks before Joseph died, he had said, "my book on Chief Joseph is . . . along toward completion. . . . The Appletons have asked for it. . . ."[22] Robert Frost's "Out, Out—" describes with painful accuracy the reactions of the chief witnesses to a young boy's death: "And they, since they were not the one dead, turned to their affairs."

Of the feelings at his death of Chief Joseph's two wives, of his other relatives, of his band, and of the Nez Perce nation as a whole, both in Washington and in Idaho, there are no direct written records and but fragmentary secondary accounts. In the large world of public affairs outside the reservations life certainly continued in its characteristic fashion. On the day of Joseph's death King Peter of Servia was crowned in the cathedral of Belgrade. On September 22 the Bank of England declared a dividend of 4½ percent. Throughout September and October a British expeditionary force was active in Tibet. On October 15, after a fierce battle on the Sha-ho River, Japanese and Russian forces faced stalement in the Russo-Japanese War. Andrew Carnegie was unanimously reelected Lord Rector of St. Andrews University, Scotland, on November 4, and four days later Theodore Roosevelt was elected to the presidency he had held since McKinley's death.

IV

Under the leadership of Judge Thomas Burke, Samuel Hill, and Meany, the University of Washington State Historical Society was energetically erecting monuments to commemorate important past events. In August, 1903, one was unveiled at Nootka, Vancouver Island, to mark the place of negotiations between Bodega y Quadra and Vancouver, and in October 1904 monuments were raised on the sites of the 1872 British and American camps on San Juan Island off the coast of Washington. Quite soon after Joseph's death, Meany, or possibly Samuel Hill, had the idea of raising one above Joseph's grave during his potlatch ceremonies. There was also again talk of disinterring Joseph's remains and reburying him, with due ceremony, in Wallowa Valley, to let him rest at last in his ancestral home. But on October 29, 1904, Steele wired Meany from Nespelem: "Council of Joseph's relatives and friends decide Joseph's remains to rest here permanently. Who defrays expense of monument if erected? They await your reply by wire. Letter follows." Steele's letter, after a prod from Meany, did follow, on November 13, 1904:

My Dear Professor

Your letter of the 10" Inst has been received and I do not blame you for calling my attention to my negligence. I have been behind in my correspondence owing to election etc. Your telegram was duly received and I have forwarded it to Chief Joseph's sister at Kamiah, Idaho. It did not reach here in time to catch them here during their visit. I have just had a consultation with Mrs. Joseph in regard to the monument. The rumor that Joseph's friends and relatives were to erect a monument is entirely erroneous. Mrs. Joseph says that she will leave all details connected with the monument with you and the Historical society. You may have any inscription you choose inscribed on the shaft. The program arranged by Joseph's people, relatives and friends is as follows: They are to meet here about the middle of next June. They will then extend the outline of their present cemetary and move Chief Joseph's remains into a new plot of ground to rest permanently. They will also have their customary feast and distribute the worldly goods of the departed Chief. They would also like to know if the monument could be completed and be here at that time so that it could be erected in connection with the other ceremonies. Do you think the monument could be here by that time? . . . There will be friends and relatives here from, all over the state, Oregon, Montana, and even from across the line and I presume the occasion will be one long to be remembered. Now Professor, the selection of the monument, inscription and other details are entirely left with you. There is one suggestion that you will kindly pardon me for making. I think it would be appropriate and proper to have an Indian head, in dress, chiseled in the granite. Have the head looking heavenward representing an attitude of appealing to the Great Father for justice. If this head could be gilded it would be a very prominent feature of the monument.

Mrs. Joseph said today that Joseph was 67 years old. This is much older than I supposed. I apprehend however, that you have all data connected with his life at your disposal, much more accurate than could be obtained from any of his friends or relatives. Any further information that you may desire either from his people or from me, kindly advise me and I shall supply it with pleasure. I would be pleased to know what kind of a monument you will select. I hope you are progressing nicely with your University work. Will be pleased to hear from you often and with many pleasant remembrances and warm personal regards

> *Truly yours*
> *Henry M. Steele*

P.S. Wasn't that an awful "storm" on the 8th Inst?

These plans, as it happened, were a pretty accurate blueprint for what eventually occurred the following summer. Meany took on the long distance planning from the University of Washington, such as ordering the monument from the New England Granite and Marble Company, Seattle, raising the money, and keeping interested whites informed of developments; E. L. Farnsworth, cashier at the State Bank of Wilbur, took on the intermediate arrangements from Wilbur, the nearest railhead and important town to Nespelem; and Steele was working on the spot.

On March 2, 1905, Steele wrote Meany to jog things along a little:

Mrs. Chief Joseph has inquired frequently as to the progress on Chief Joseph's monument. Also, if I ever hear from you. They are already discussing the arrangements of the final ceremonies over Chief Joseph. I look for a very large assemblage of Indians here in June, to witness the last rites. Is the monument under way, now? We are just experiencing a little spring sunshine and the weather is extremely plesant. How are you progressing with your work? I presume your winter's work has been somewhat arduous. My wife little daughter and myself are well. . . .

On April 7 Samuel Hill dashed off a note to Meany saying that June 20 would be a good date for him to attend a ceremony at Nespelem and asking Meany to "get figures" for the cost of the monument. In response to Meany's urging of June 20 as the best date, Steele—after reporting, on May 1, initial indecision among the Indians due to Red Thunder's absence—was able to say on May 5 that "Mrs. Joseph, Red Thunder and other members of the tribe have selected June 20" as the day for erecting the monument over Chief Joseph." In the same letter he outlined plans for transporting the monument the fifty miles from Wilbur by wagon and suggested formal press announcements in local papers of the date set for the ceremonies. Hill telegraphed Meany on May 13 that he would advance the Society $175 to erect the monument in its name. So almost everything was set to go, and this was confirmed by Steele in a letter of May 22 in which he informed Meany that he had interviewed Mrs. Chief Joseph "and she is perfectly satisfied in every way. Inscriptions, and all details are perfectly satisfactory to all."

Meany accordingly sent his final instructions to the New England Granite and Marble Company.[23]

Besides the portrait of Chief Joseph as arranged, the inscriptions on the monument ordered are as follows:

CHIEF JOSEPH

in raised letters on the base.
   On one side of the shaft:
      Hin-mah-too-yah-lat-kekt
      Thunder rolling in the mountains
   On another side of the shaft:
      He led his people in the Nez Perce war of 1877.
      Died, 21 September, 1904. Age, about 60 years.
   On the back of shaft:
      Erected 20 June, 1905, by the Washington
      University State Historical Society
The time is now precious as we must get this monument into Wilbur in time to allow the Indians to transport it 50 miles in wagons before 19 June.
Dont delay an hour from this time.

                       Yours faithfully
                       Edmond S. Meany

On the same day Meany wrote to Steele with questions about a possible potlatch:

Is it the intention of the widow and friends to make a potlatch as in the case of Chief Moses?

If so I would like to see Mr. Samuel Hill properly remembered. He is paying the cost of this monument in the name of the Society. He also paid the deficit for Joseph's visit to Seattle. He liked the Chief and would appreciate a keepsake.

I am willing to confess that I am not free from such a desire myself. Joseph's "Eagle Hat" will probably go to his successor. I would cherish one of his Buffalo robes the rest of my life. If there is to be a potlatch you might talk this over with Mrs. Joseph, but if there is to be no potlatch don't mention it to her.[24]

On May 28 Steele suggested that Meany send a formal invitation to Indian Agent John McA. Webster, "a very estimable gentleman," and asked a flurry of queries about cement, transport, and other technicalities.[25] The following letters reveal the degree to which he was involved in the minutiae of arrangements:

June 2" 1905

Dear Professor:—

Your two letters under date of the 26" and 27" ultimo has reached me and I fully note their contents. If Mr. Farnsworth will let me know the date of the arrival of the monument at Wilbur, I will see that its transportation is properly attended to. We have two small flags here, none of them large enough to cover shaft. I will drop Mr. Farnsworth a note and ask him to loan us a flat from Wilbur for the occasion. If we cannot get a suitable one in Wilbur, we could use the 2 small ones here. I think it would be very advisable to send a sack of cement along with the monument, then we will be sure to have it. They seem to have it in Wilbur but [only] in large quantities. I will have the C. of Indians to fire the volley as you suggest. There is no music here but as I expect quite a number of white people here, I presume they would be willing to join in some national song as you suggest. I had consultation with Albert Watters [sic] (acting chief) and Mrs. Joseph yesterday in reference to a potlatch. Mrs. Joseph said that all Joseph's clothes would go to his nephew and other relations. But I have arranged that you and Mr. Hill will not be forgotten. I explained how kind you both had been to Joseph and she has promised me that you both would be remembered. . . . I will see that the cemetary is nicely cleaned and I cannot see now, why the ceremonies should not be a grand success. Indians are now arriving from Montana and from appearances there will be an immense crowd. . . .

Very sincerely
Henry M. Steele

Nespilem, Wash June 8" 1905

Dear Professor:—

Everything is moving along well at this end of the line but I have not heard anything about the arrival of monument at, Wilbur. Some of the Indians are arriving from Idaho and I expect quite a crowd. I have sent to Mr. Farnsworth for a flag. . . . [and] have not heard from Mr. Farnsworth as yet. I had another consultation with the Nez Perces on Tuesday. They will have a big feast on the 21st. Incidentally I arranged for something for both you and Mr. Hill. I think you will get your buffalo robe. Al-okot is sick in Spokane but we hope he will be able to be here in time. The election of a new chief will take place after the feast. I arranged for firing the guns and the Company of Indians will all appear in their Indian dress. I am sending you under separate cover the Spokane Chronicle in which appears an article from Lew Wilmot. He was a member of the volunteer party sent against Joseph in '77. It should be answered and hope you will do so. I am well acquainted with Wilmot and know him to be very much biased and prejudiced against Joseph. He is about 70 years old and in his dotage. I see no reason now why every thing should not be a success. Write me any suggestions you wish carried out. With pleasant remembrances

Sincerely Yours
Henry M. Steele

And, in a letter of June 11, Meany invited himself to stay, seemingly not as a paying guest, in the hotel run by Steele's wife.

You will know a corner for me in case of a crowded house and for the rest I don't give a whoop. Cheese and crackers are good enough. . . . [In the ceremony] I wish to subordinate myself as much as possible and if there is anyone available to make the address we will hand that job over to him. I will be ready in case I am needed. All I want is to make the day a success.[26]

Despite the temporary loss of the monument in transit, everything proceeded with gratifying smoothness: Indians were coming in from all over the Plateau and Plains; the monument was paid for ($175.00), as was the cost of shipping it ($18.85); numbers of white well-wishers began to put in an appearance; and Meany published "Highest Type of Indian" in the *Seattle Times* of June 13 as a refutation of Lew Wilmot's attacks.

And the U.S. Indian Service was proving cooperative. Agent Webster replied to Meany's invitation as follows:

I thank you heartily for the kindly words and the personal invitation, just received, to be present during the ceremonies incident to the dedication of a monument to the late Chief Joseph at Nespilem.

Last Fall I promised the Nez Perces to be with them on the occasion of their election of a successor to Joseph, and as this event immediately follows the dedicatory ceremonies I will have the pleasure of meeting you at the place where this great Chief spent the last, and not the happiest, years of his life.

You may command me in any matter wherein I can be of service to you personally or in the prosecution of your official researches.[27]

Webster had indeed made a promise to the Nez Perces. In a letter of May 23 to the acting chief, Albert Waters, he had accepted an invitation to the election ceremonies, "Hoping and believing that your people will choose a worthy successor to the lamented Joseph and that the ceremony may be conducted with the dignity and order due to the memory of that distinguished chieftain."[28] And, despite the fact that he took steps to *ensure* "dignity and order" by requesting Thomas McCrossen, on the same day, to arrange for the provision of U.S. deputy marshals in the event of trouble, Webster did hold Joseph in high regard. Earlier, in January 1905, he had tried to collect relics of the chief for display at the Lewis and Clark Exposition in Portland and later, as will be seen, he wrote appreciatively of Joseph to at least one outsider.

Dr. Latham hoped to have a monopoly on pictures, saying to Meany, "The Indians are peculiar about being Photographed and I have been thinking it would be best for you not to bring any Photographer with you. I think we can manage them best by ourselves. I have plenty of plates and will make anything in that line you may wish."[29] But his wish was not to be requited. Already, on May 30, Lee Moorhouse of Pendleton, Oregon, a former army officer and Indian agent, a man who had exhibited his pictures at the St. Louis Exposition of 1904, had written to Meany to say that he and his camera would be there. Moorhouse had good reasons for wishing to be present: he had become friendly with Joseph when the chief visited the Umatilla Reservation in 1890; he had made some fine portraits of Joseph, and one of his pictures had served as the model for the carving of Joseph's face on the monument about to be erected. In fact, on the very day that Dr. Latham expressed his hope that other photographers would be kept away, Meany announced in the press that both Major Moorhouse and Dr. Latham would be there. And, of course, as it happened, Curtis was there too.

The actual event, which got properly underway on June 20, was not without its worries for Meany (he had had to wire back home from Lester for his spectacles to be sent on to Wilbur and he afterwards left his cigars behind), but the press reported the occasion as a successful one. Spokane's *Spokesman Review* for Thursday, June 22, printed a story on the election of Albert Waters as chief and on the unveiling ceremony, while the issue of Friday, June 23, carried a reporter's version of Lee Moorhouse's description of these events, and two days later the paper put out a detailed description of the potlatch ceremonies in which, apparently, Henry Steele was "among the lucky ones." As might be expected, Meany's unsigned articles for the *Post-Intelligencer* gave much detail: in one titled "Nespilem Indians Receive Monument," he reviewed events leading up to that point and some of the monument's adventures in reaching Nespelem; in "Waters Succeeds Joseph," in which Waters was referred to as "a typical blanket Indian," he presented some of the political strife the Nez Perces were suffering as a result of Joseph's death;[30] and his article entitled "Unveil Monument" was his version of the dedication ceremony. In the course of this last mentioned report Meany described how the older Indians objected to the presence of photographers and how, after "two hours of parley," only the soothing presence of Captain Webster had calmed their fears. He noted that Yellow Bull, Albert Waters, and Ess-ko-ess had delivered speeches; that "Professor Meany traced the life of Chief Joseph in the only address by a white man"; and that E. L. Farnsworth and Howard Spining began and concluded the ceremonies—over which Henry Steele had "presided"—with an "invocation" and a "benediction," respectively. The unveiling itself "was done by four Nez Perce boys stationed each at a lodge pole planted in the ground. At a signal they hoisted the draped American flag which was then suspended as a canopy from the lodge poles." It was under this that the speakers had stood.[31]

Meany ended this report with the note that "prominent among the photogra-

phers present" were Curtis, Moorhouse, and Latham. The most prominent of
these experienced (if a reporter's account is to be believed) more than just the
"two hours of parley" that Meany's article mentioned; in a story filed on Curtis'
return from his 1905 summer field trip, the following paragraphs appeared:

*Incidentally, however, Mr. Curtis encountered a great deal of trouble in the
Nez Perce country. That particular tribe is torn asunder over the successor to
the late Chief Joseph.*

*"A contemptible, ignorant, lazy loafer," to quote Mr. Curtis literally, by the
name of Albert Waters, is trying to take the place of the late ruler, and for
some reason he conceived the idea that Curtis was bad medicine and refused
to let him take photos of the unveiling of the Joseph monument.*

*Albert Waters walked up to the Curtis camera and pushed it roughly aside
just as the local artist was about to press the button. Naturally that made Edward
somewhat angry. He restrained himself, however, and, looking the Indian squarely
in the eyes, delivered himself of the following:*

*"Albert, if you lay your hands on that camera again I will feel compelled to
punch your face, and if that is not sufficient I will blow the top of your head
off," and so saying he pulled a saucy little six-shooter out of his pocket, whereupon
Albert Waters quit like a dog. Turning to Big Bull or Little Bull, or whichever
member of the Bull family it was that was an eye witness to the affair, Curtis
said:*

"Bull, what do you think of Albert Waters?"

*"Oh," replied Bull, "you pick 'em up old sock, and wash him and make
him chief. All same Albert Waters."*

*"The unveiling of the Joseph monument," said Mr. Curtis, "was really a very
pretty ceremony. Albert Waters got up and attempted to make a speech, but
his remarks were received in silence. When Little Bull [sic] arose, however, he
received the closest attention, and when he told the story of Joseph's life in the
simple language of the red man the many war widows present set up a great
wailing.* "[32]

It is perhaps not surprising that when Curtis came to write his own account
of the ceremonies as a brief part of one of a series of illustrated articles on
"Vanishing Indian Types," which he contributed to *Scribner's Magazine* in 1906,
no mention was made of any such incident:

*In June of last year I went into the hills of the Okanogan country in eastern
Washington. The occasion of my going was the reburial of the splendid old
Nez Perce chief, Joseph, and the erection of a man-fashioned monument at what
it is hoped will be his final resting-place.*

*Matters dragged in the digging of one grave and the digging out of another.
It was no small task, and, hoping to expedite matters, I dug, pried, tugged, and
hefted in assisting to get that burial chest out of one place and moved to another.*

It was what one might term a study in practical or applied ethnology. Many speeches were made. A college professor in frock coat and silk hat did part of the talking. Several chiefs and would-be chiefs in blankets and feathers did the rest. We did not have the regular Indian burial rite in the reburial. The Indians said: "Last year we buried him, this time just move him." A child died early that morning, and the Indians buried it in their own way late in the afternoon. In this there was no "Boston hat" or "Boston man's talk," but a most beautiful pagan ceremony. The mourners encircled the grave. A high-keyed, falsetto chant by forty voices, rising and falling in absolute unison, sent chills down our spines that hot June day, as does the dismal wail of wintry winds in the pine forests.

On the following day came the Chief Joseph potlatch—a Hi-u *potlatch (Big Giving), in which every earthly possession of the old chief and his wife was given away. Through it all the wife sat by the side of the great stack of goods being distributed, handing out each article and trinket. At times when some article obviously dear to her heart was handed out great tears would roll down her cheeks. Two days were taken in this giving, and then the visiting Indians tore down the grand council lodge, and so closed the last chapter in the life and death of the most decent Indian the Northwest has ever known. No more will he beg of the Great White Father, and say: "All I ask is to go back to the old home in the Wallowa Valley; my father's home, and the home of my father's father." His troubled life has run its course, and one of the greatest Indians who ever lived is no longer a part of the white man's burden.*[33]

When Curtis sat down to write of these things for the Nez Perce section of *The North American Indian*, published in 1911, he gave an historical sketch largely devoted to the war of 1877. Unlike Meany, he did not credit Joseph with a major role as a general, but saw him, rather, as a spiritual leader, and concluded the sketch with some remarks on the chief's end:

Joseph continued through the remainder of his life at Nespilem the hopeless plea for the Wallowa Valley, one of his last acts being a journey to Washington in one more effort. Perhaps it was discouragement, more likely it was intuition, but at any rate he seemed to know that his life was drawing to a close, for while returning to his home he told those with whom he talked that he would make no more journeys: he would soon be gone. And so it was. In the following year, on September 21, 1904, his life's fight closed.

The summer following Joseph's death the writer visited Nespilem, to be present at the "Joseph potlatch"—the giving away of all his earthly possessions. A large "long house"—made of many tipis joined together—was erected for the occasion, and into it was taken such property as the old chief had collected in the last years of his life. There was a great quantity of these personal belongings, since, owing to Joseph's prominence, he had received many gifts from both white people and Indians, and in addition his relatives from Lapwai had brought a great number of new blankets, that the occasion might be creditable to the family. The collected material made a formidable heap at one end of the large lodge, and two days were consumed in its distribution. The widow sat at one side of the pile, and, taking up articles singly, handed them to the crier, at the same time announcing through him the name of the intended recipient. This was continued until every possession was given away, even to the trifling articles of the widow's work basket, and the simplest household utensils.

This was the closing act in the drama of the life of Joseph, the last of the Nez Perce "non-treaty" chiefs. To employ words in condemnation of the great wrong that his people suffered would be useless, for was it not but one of the countless iniquities that have marked the white man's dealings with the Indians since the landing of the Pilgrims at Plymouth?[34]

"There is no such thing as history, only histories," E. H. Carr has said, and by the time Curtis in his old age, in 1950, came to record his memory of these memorial ceremonies for Joseph, it was not the dignity of the potlatch he most remembered but the effort involved in the reburial. In a letter to Harriet Leitch, formerly of the Seattle Public Library, he wrote: "In the Days of Long Ago I helped bury the Chief twice. In order to bury him the second time we had to dig him up: I did most of the digging. It was a very hot day and The Noble Red Men said 'let the white men do the digging. They know how.' Professor Meany and Sam Hill participated in the reburial. The Professor wrote a good story of the reburial."[35] Much nearer to the time, Curtis' chief assistant, William W. Phillips, his nephew by marriage, reminisced: "The major problem of the job of digging—and we had to dig deep—was done in the early afternoon by the speaker of the day, Three Knives Meany, Edward S. Curtis and the writer. Indians did, however, dig the new hole, and it is well that they did, for I know a man or two who wouldn't be here to tell the tale if the pale faces had had to wrestle with another ton of gravel on that scorching day."[36]

The "good story" that Curtis said Meany composed is most likely the one dated June 24, which, illustrated with Latham photographs, appeared in the *Post-Intelligencer* of Sunday, June 25, 1905, under the title "The Reburial of Chief Joseph":

. . . Relays of Nez Perce young men dug the new grave large and deep, with the head facing the monument toward the east. But when it came to dig up the remains from the old grave the Indians needed the help of the white men, who willingly gave it.

Last Look at Old Chief

With pathetic simplicity the Nez Perces asked the privilege of opening the coffin so the relatives and friends of the dead chief might again look upon his face. The whites stood back while the Nez Perces circled around the body of

Joseph. Tears fell from the eyes of old warriors, while the widows of the war time gave voice to the wail of the grieving Indian.

By noon the reburial was accomplished, and it was agreed that the Indians and whites would return at 2 P.M. for the unveiling of the monument. Through correspondence it had been agreed that a dozen Nez Perces, clad in war suits of buckskin, should fire a volley over the grave at the conclusion of a parade of all the Nez Perces and their friends. When the older Indians arrived on the ground they explained that the traditions of the tribe would not permit such gay or noisy demonstrations on the solemn occasion of a reburial. Both the parade and the firing of a volley was therefore abandoned.

The proverbial slowness of the Indian was again made evident, for it was 4 P.M. when the Indians arrived. The three selected to make addresses in unveiling the monument came dressed in all the splendor of Indian war bonnets.

APPEARANCE OF YELLOW BULL

Yellow Bull, almost blind, rode a fine horse and made an impressive appearance. He was also the greatest orator among the assembled Indians. His first appearance set the widows of the war wailing, for they saw in his bold face and his war dress so much that reminded them of the tragic past. After the ceremonies the address of Yellow Bull was translated by Camille Williams, a full-blooded Nez Perce, who has proved himself an excellent interpreter. The address was as follows:

"I am very glad to meet you all today, my bothers and sisters and my white friends. When the Creator made us He put us on this earth, as the flowers on the land, and He takes us all in His arms and keeps us in peace and friendship. Our friendship and peace shall never fade, but it will shine forever. Our people love our old customs. I am very glad to see our white friends here attending this ceremony, and it seems like we all have the same sad feelings, and that fact helps to wipe away my tears for the loss of our dead chief.

"Joseph is dead, but his words will live forever. This monument will stand for many, many years. Joseph's words will stand as long as the monument.

"We are both, the red and the white, here, and the Great Spirit looks down on us both and now if we are good and live right, like Joseph, we shall see Him."

CHIEF ALBERT'S ADDRESS

There was no doubt of this man's actual chieftainship. His every word and gesture indicated that fact. The newly elected chief of the Nez Perces at Nespilem is a much younger man in years and experience. His address at the unveiling of the monument was his first public appearance. He spoke very briefly as follows:

"Now, dear friends, we meet here. We people were born, and you people were born. Each one knows his own customs. Today I take my stand in the place of our old chief and today all of you stand with me in that presence."

The new chief has elected to be known as Chief Albert. He was followed on *this occasion by Ess-Kow-Ess, one of the most prominent spokesmen of his tribe, who spoke as follows:*

"I am very glad to meet all you people—that is, the Indians and the whites. When the world was made—we both know the One that made this world. When it was finished, the same One gave man growth.

"And out of this land the law was made for both of us, red and white.

"And this man, our Old Chief Joseph, is dead, but then his words are not dead. And for this same reason the law of the soul is the same for both of us.

"For that reason we elect this new Albert chief, which suits us who know him.

"I have finished."

Prof. Edmond S. Meany, of course, addressed himself to the whites in reviewing the life of Chief Joseph. However, not a few of the Indians followed much of his speech. Descendants of the chiefs whose names he mentioned came to him afterward to talk about those men. . . .

The Chief Joseph Potlatch

The word potlatch is not in common use among the Indians here. When they refer to it they call it a feast and usually it commemorates the dead. Among the Puget sound and West Coast Indians a live man becomes great by making many potlatches. The Chief Joseph potlatch took place Friday. It was one of the greatest affairs of the kind we have any record of. The huge council lodge was filled. At the head of the lodge were gathered heaps of the worldly possessions of the late Chief Joseph. Around these sat his three nephews—Ollicut, of Montana; Black Eagle, of Lapwai, and Chief Tow-at-Way, of the Umatillas. In the only chair in the lodge sat the official announcer, Pio-pio mox-mox, "Yellow Bird," who is one of the noted men of the tribe. At his right hand on the ground sat Chief Joseph's younger widow. Back of these relatives sat the blind chief, Yellow Bull. From this end of the long tepee or council lodge were ranged the men, all reclining on reed mats and robed in brilliant blankets for nearly half the length of the lodge, and beyond the men were the women and children.

Much the same arrangement had prevailed during the big feast at noon. Elaborate preparations had been made for that feast. It was by no means a jolly affair, but all were welcome and there was plenty of all things that Indians enjoy at their big feasts.

Speech From Horseback

After dinner speeches were made, the crowning one of which was made by Chief Yellow Bull. This speech was made on horseback, while the old chief rode slowly three times around the outside of the big council lodge. He rode Chief Joseph's faithful old horse and besides that dignity he wore all of Chief Joseph's war clothes, including the famous eagle-feather war-bonnet. His speech related almost wholly to the greatness of the man whose horse he was riding and whose clothes he was wearing.

If the newly elected Chief Albert had been one of the old warriors of Chief Joseph's band, it is quite likely that he would have filled the role played by Yellow Bull, but Albert is a young man, while Yellow Bull is a warrior, now the most famous among the survivors of the Nez Perces. He lives at Lapwai, and it looks as if he will carry with him the head chieftainship so long enjoyed by Chief Joseph at Nespilem. . . . There was considerable friction over the election of Albert as chief. Leaders of the tribe had gone to Capt. John McA. Webster, the agent at Miles, and asked him to be present at the election on June 20 to see fair play. Then without a stated reason they changed and elected Albert Waters on June 15, before Capt. Webster could get word of their purpose. . . . As Peo-peo-tah-like, Yellow Bull and other candidates, with their friends, arrived from Lapwai and elsewhere they complained bitterly that the election had been pulled off before the stated time. . . . No one has been able to fathom the real reason for the haste in choosing Albert as chief. It looks as if his friends were afraid to wait for the arrival of the others of the tribe. The leaders gave out as the reason that they needed some one to preside at the ceremonies and to lead Chief Joseph's horse in the parade. Yet after his election Albert was not permitted to do these things, so it was simply a course of his friends landing him in the place by rather questionable methods. He is now the chief and he may develop into a useful officer for his people. He is, like Joseph, a perfectly moral and upright man. Thus far he has declined to allow his picture to be taken.

After Yellow Bull had made his speech on horseback the Indians gathered in the big lodge and began the wailing for the dead. At the conclusion of the crying a number of speeches were made. Some of these were by the Nespilem Indians, whose language is different from the Nez Perce. David Williams, a typical Nez Perce, interpreted promptly and with force. This incident brought the past vividly to view.

Then followed the giving away of Chief Joseph's property. Nearly every Indian present was given something. The great war bonnets and war clothing went to the three nephews. A dozen watches were among the gifts, three fine guns and an endless array of blankets. One of the three buffalo robes was given to Three Knives or Prof. Meany. . . .

Potlatch Continues Saturday

It was supposed that the potlatch of Chief Joseph's property was concluded last evening, but this morning the Indians again gathered in the big council tepee for more speeches, and then all the household goods and great piles of food were given away. Sacks of flour were opened and given away, a portion to each squaw. Meats, bread, syrup, dishes and table utensils were all freely distributed.

More speeches followed, and then Chief Joseph's huge bass drum, which had been given to the newly elected Chief Albert, was brought into the tepee and soon there appeared with war whoops and yelling ten young men in gala attire, with one older warrior, who was almost nude. These men gave a war dance, while the women wept over the memory of the past thus portrayed. During a rest in the dance an old warrior, suitably bedecked with furs and feathers and carrying in his hand a calumet, gave an oration in the Nez Perce language. This dancing was the crowning and concluding event of the Chief Joseph funeral.

Immediately afterward interpreters for the ten languages represented in the council became busy over preparations for the celebration of the Fourth of July including the extensive programme of horse races.

In order to write his good stories for the press, Meany made meticulous notes. These he kept, presumably for later use in his biography of Joseph. Thus it is that his records of the ceremonies for the dead chief survive among his voluminous papers: copies, in Camille Williams' hand, of the speeches of Yellow Bull, Ess-ko-ess, and Albert Waters; notes on Albert (he was thirty-five, had lived at Nespelem for twenty years, had been married for seventeen years, and owned thirty-five horses and two hundred cattle); a list recording the distribution at the potlatch of some of the significant items owned by Joseph, such as his blanket and shirt to Yellow Bull, his gun and calumet to Albert; a myth in both rough draft and polished versions that was told to him and to William Phillips; and several other, more fragmentary items. Also, even out in the field Meany kept up his barrage of letters to friends and to people he wished to impress. Thus on June 26 he wrote to Samuel Hill, who had, apparently, not been able to stay in Nespelem for the potlatch part of the ceremonies, giving a brief account of things to date. "Only three white men were honored," he said, "you, Mr. Steele and myself. Your present was an old beaded purse that Chief Joseph had used for years. I am today mailing it to you. . . . Mr. Steele also received a bead-work present. I received an old-time buffalo robe. Although the hair is worn off in spots I shall always prize the gift as one of the evidences of the Chief's life of long ago."[27]

Later in the summer he told Hill of his season's work among the Indians for *Post-Intelligencer* articles, adding that he had taken over one hundred and fifty photographs. Considering all this writing activity and the fact that so much of it has been preserved, it is surprising that no record at all of Meany's own speech at the unveiling ceremony seems to have survived. His oration was doubtless long and delivered with flourish, but its contents must remain conjectural. On the other hand, some indication of the sentiment underlying it may be had from a short piece titled "Tenderness of an Indian Chief." This is one item from a book-length unpublished typescript found among Meany's papers of a work to be called "Western Miniatures":

Chief Joseph, the Nez Perce, was the greatest Indian leader of the far west. After his conquest in 1877 he was held by the Government practically as a prisoner of war until his death (1904). He was given a large farm and buildings were erected for him at Nespilem on the Colville Reservation. He was not happy on a farm and soon left it for a tepee on the bank of the little river. That slender dwelling of canvas and lodgepoles became the real capitol of the Nez Perce nation.

His fame brought him many gifts and keepsakes from soldiers and men of prominence. While his guest at Nespilem, I was shown many of these and was pleased to see among them pictures and letters from Generals Howard, Miles, Gibbon, and others who had fought against him.

A package wrapped in a buffalo robe was brought to the center of the tepee. It contained a little chest in which was a hundred or more photographs. He knew them all and told of his experiences on the warpath with the soldiers. A little picture he held on one brown palm while he fondly stroked it with the other. He spoke from his scant supply of English words: "Good woman".

Other pictures were shown but three times he came back to the little one of the "Good woman". Asking to see it, I found written on the back: "To Chief Joseph from his loving daughter Sarah". I knew that Joseph's children had all died and there I saw an Indian's heart greater in a father's grief than in a warrior's glory.[38]

V

Joseph's death created a vacuum of power—or, more properly, of influence—among the Nez Perces. Old rivalries reemerged; new factions, which had been partly caused by the placement of the people on different reservations, formed and hardened; people of different Christian sects opposed one another; men and women who adhered to the ways of their ancestors became more openly contemptuous of those who struggled to farm in the manner of the whites; the "progressives" felt that with the death of Joseph a new era should begin.

Soon after Joseph's death reports emanating from Nespelem began to appear in the press. A typical one was by Vella Winner in *The Oregon Sunday Journal* of Portland for Christmas Day 1904. Titled "Choosing Chief Joseph's Successor," it examined the claims upon the chieftainship, or at least the alleged claims, of such men as Peo-peo Tholekt (characterized as "a politician and a schemer"), Ollicott ("the choice of the Montana and Idaho Indians"), David Williams ("an intelligent and diplomatic Indian"), and Willie Andrews ("a cousin of Chief Joseph"), finally plumping for Andrews as the most likely successor. The source of the information in this article—other than a Carlisle Indian School graduate, Samuel Tilden, who was quoted at length—was probably Edward Latham, whose pictures were used as illustrations. Certainly, the appointment of Albert Waters did not settle matters.

The situation was further complicated by the fact that in a change of policy bent on breaking traditional patterns even more, the Bureau of Indian Affairs no longer recognized chiefs as such, and Webster was constrained to point this out to the newly elected chief in a letter of June 30, 1905. (He did soften the blow, however, by adding "there will be no objection to my recognising you as a leading [sic] or representative of your people."[39]) As the comment attributed to Yellow Bull—"you pick 'em up old sock, and wash him and make him chief"—indicates, as soon as Albert Waters assumed the chieftainship he met opposition from various hostile groups. Meany reported briefly on this turmoil in "Yellow Bird Scouts," the last of his unsigned *Post-Intelligencer* items on the Nez Perces before he moved on to spend the summer traveling among many of the other Indian peoples of the state of Washington. "Yellow Bird Scouts" appeared on June 30 and told how Yellow Bird, a prominent and wealthy Idaho Nez Perce felt that Albert was too young and too slight in every way to fill the post he had assumed and that he, Yellow Bird, acting with the consent and knowledge of many of the senior men of the tribe, would be testing allegiances in order to secure instead the appointment of either Ollicott or Black Eagle.

Similar unrest was to occur periodically for years to come, but when Steele wrote to Meany the following February, the reservation was relatively peaceful:

My Dear Professor:—

I take more than ordinary pleasure in acknowledging the receipt of your hand-some and appropriate gift to our little baby girl, which reached me last night by registered mail. My language is inadequate in expressing my sentiments in thanking you for your very kind remembrance.

We do not appreciate the present so much intrinsically as we do the spirit which prompted its giving. . . . Our little girl's Conception of such a beautiful present is, as yet entirely vague but we shall be delighted in telling her in later years who it was, that remembered her so kindly in her infancy.

She is a smart, sweet and clever little child and I must confess that we are justly proud and passionately fond of her.

Myself and wife are both very well and we have had a quiet winter thus far. We expect quite a stir here during the coming summer. I presume you had a successful year in your college work and sincerely hope that you and family are enjoying the blessings of good health. Chief Albert Watters [sic] has just returned from a visit to the Capital City. I have not seen him since his return.[40]

But there were troubles and worries over relations with the outer world, espe-cially over government monies, a cause in which Amos Wilkinson—who was, he claimed, "the nearest blood relation to Chief Joseph"—tried to elicit Meany's support in a letter of December 31, 1905, which he then followed on January 11, 1906 with a brief report on his own efforts in Washington, D.C. (He also asked for further assistance in February 1906 after the failure of the Moscow National Bank, Idaho, where the Nez Perces had deposits.) Meany did try to help, first by stressing to Wilkinson that to make any effective claim he must take full documentation to Washington, and second by writing to Commissioner F. E. Leupp as one whose "interest has been aroused while studying [Nez Perce] history."[41] But the response was only a long letter fom Leupp rejecting the Nez Perce claims in the familiar legalistic Bureau of Indian Affairs style.

Agent Webster was more personal. He was interested in the Nez Perces and their history and had appreciated the ceremonies for Joseph, as may be seen in his letter dated June 24, 1905, to N. C. Titus, a western history buff from Helena, Montana. He said, in part:

The occasion of my visit [to Nespelem] was the dedication on June 20th or [sic] a monument to Joseph, erected by the Washington State Historical Society, the ceremonies in connection with which were most interesting and the event probably the last of its kind that will occur. Several hundred Indians, including visitors from other Reservations, and about one hundred whites were present, addresses being made by three Nez Perce Chiefs and Mr. E. S. Meany, Professor of History in the Washington State University. Among the distinguished Indians was old Yellow Bull, second in command during Joseph's famous retreat before the United States forces. . . .[42]

Webster was also deeply involved in efforts to secure some financial restitution to the Indians of a number of tribes under his jurisdiction for monies diverted from them as a result of the activities of former agent Albert M. Anderson. Webster believed that Anderson had used the influence of his official position to obtain guardianships over Indian children for his own profit, and it is certain that Anderson was removed from his post after an investigation found that he had forged the names on an entire annuity payment voucher, apparently collecting the money himself. And when his accounts were cleared after his departure, a shortage of over $6,000 in government money was discovered, which his bonding company had to pay.

Meany was most impressed by Webster's dedication to his work and published an unsigned report on the subject in the *Post-Intelligencer* of Sunday, July 9, 1905, titled "Captain Webster Loves His Work." Something of this background is apparent in the letter Webster wrote to Meany at the end of 1906:

U.S. Indian Agency

Miles, Wash., Dec. 5th" 1906.

Dear Professor:

As the Governor of North Carolina said to the Governor of South Carolina anent the subject of "drinks," "it's a long time between our letters," and I was more than pleased a few days ago to find on my desk a copy of the first number of the "Washington Historical Quarterly. Edmund S. Meany, Managing Editor."

You can count on me as a member of the Society from this date and you will find inclosed my check for $2.25 (25 for possible exchange), subscription for the first year.

I have just returned from Washington City, having been summoned there by the Dept. of Justice to assist in preventing a steal of $225,000.00 from the Colville Indians by some rascally attorneys who succeeded in getting a bill through

Congress last Spring authorizing them to take their claim before the Court of Claims. And such a claim!—that it was through their efforts before committees of congress during the first twelve years that the "McLaughlin Agreement" of last winter was, in the main features, ratified by Congress last Spring, and denying that the long continued efforts of the Secretary of the Interior and Commissioner of Indian Affairs had any influences with that body! They allege a contract with the Colvilles—two contracts—one for ten years, made in 1894 and procured through gross fraud; another made in November 1904, manufactured outright by Ex-Agent A. M. Anderson, by perjury, forgery, and additional false swearing concerning it when recently placed upon the witness stand in regard to the matter. If he does not land in the penitentiary it will be solely because of a total failure of justice.

I am still plodding away—and enjoying my work as much as ever. Yes, the more I see of most white men the better I like Indians. Sad, but true.

Try to arrange for a little visit with me next Spring, or summer. Perhaps we can go over to Nespilem and witness the Fourth of July festivities. In any case, and at any time, I will be delighted to renew our acquaintance, so pleasantly begun. Bring a friend or two with you and they will be heartily welcomed.

With best wishes for a happy Holiday season and New Year.

Very Sincerely Yours,
Jno. McA. Webster.

Meanwhile, Edmond Meany himself was involved in a host of other things; he worked on a kind of documentary history of the United States and both initiated and completed his book entitled *History of the State of Washington* (1909). But he was certainly reminded of the Nez Perces. In the autumn of 1905 Barnett Stillwell succeeded in soliciting his help in what proved to be his futile efforts to become agent responsible for the allocation of lands— to both Indians and whites—on the Colville reservation in the event of its being legally thrown open for white settlement. On September 12, 1905, Steele wrote on behalf of Mrs. Chief Joseph to ask for the return of a picture she had let the historian borrow, and on October 30 she dictated a letter to Steele for Meany requesting an enlargement of the picture he had just returned! (She sent him a further reminder the following March.) Meany was also helping Edward Curtis—who had moved on, temporarily at least, to other tribes—with his work on the Teton Sioux: in the field he helped gather ethnological data, and in the study he wrote most of the "Historical Sketch," for the Sioux volume.

Curtis was working furiously to amass material for the first three volumes of *The North American Indian*, due to be published in 1907, and, as is clear from his letters to Meany at that time, he suffered severe doubts about the ability of his various assistants to live up to his expectations. Meany, of course, encouraged Curtis generally and in particular agreed to write a piece publicizing *The North American Indian* enterprise for a major journal of that time, *The World's Work*, edited by Walter Hines Page. He perhaps saw, too, that the Seattle studio really was not always as efficient as it might have been while Curtis was out in the field. In connection with the Nez Perces, for instance, Amos Wilkinson communicated with him from Lapwai, Idaho, on behalf of one of Curtis' principal Nez Perce informants, Three Eagles, asking for pictures that had been promised. On August 17, 1905, W. W. Phillips wrote from the Curtis Studio seeking Meany's help in sorting out the addresses of Indians who had been promised photographs, a subject on which he suffered further exchanges with Curtis operatives in January and June of 1906.

From Anderson Meany seems to have heard nothing in the years after 1904; from Latham nothing after 1908.

In the fall of 1907, in response to a request from John Watermelon Redington (a friend and former Indian fighter) that he furnish some notes to Cyrus Townsend Brady, who was working on a biography of Joseph, Meany implied that he was frequently in touch with the Nez Perces and indicated that it was still his intention to write his own life of the chief. But to Brady, who was author of the "American Fights and Fighters Series," including *Northwestern Fights and Fighters*, which features the Nez Perce War of 1877, Meany did give several paragraphs on Joseph's last years. Most of this was material copied from his thesis, but he also included the following personal memory: "Chief Joseph appreciated a sympathetic friend. When I was about to leave him he took my hand and bestowed upon me the Indian name Metaht Wultz meaning 'Three Knives' and now whenever I visit the Nez Perces they know me by that name alone."[43]

The unwritten biography of Joseph can hardly have troubled Meany in later years—he was so active in so many spheres that he could never be accused of shirking his responsibilities—but it must have been with some poignancy that he received a letter dated in April 1927 from Barnett Stillwell, the man through whom Joseph's letters had been transmitted to him nearly thirty years earlier.[44]

BARNETT STILLWELL
REAL ESTATE LOANS INSURANCE
CORRESPONDENCE SOLICITED

Jerome, Idaho

April 30th. 1927.

Prof. Edward S. Meaney [sic]
U. of W.
Seattle. Wash.

My dear Prof. I don't suppose you have written that life of Joseph yet. You have several pictures of my little girl with Joseph and I am deeply interested in them, very much so and am anxious to get some of them. Now Prof. when are you going to have some of them printed. I would like about two dozen. One dozen of each and if you can get them taken I would be glad to pay for them or, if you could send them to me I would have them taken here and return the proofs to you.

I noticed by the papers awhile back that an immense statue of Joseph was being planned.

Your little interpretor is living at Cottage Grove, Oreg. Her name is Mrs. Frank Dickson. I plan to surprise her with those pictures.

With kindest personal regards.
Barnett Stillwell

Henry Steele also kept in touch with Meany. In 1906 he tried to help in the identification of figures in a photograph, sent Meany best wishes from several Indians, and reported that, thanks to "kind Providence," his wife and daughter were "hearty and happy."[45] By this time Steele's daughter Irene was a toddler and, as the only white child in the small colony of whites at Nespelem, she was much loved by everyone. She was also readily accepted by the Indians and enjoyed an intimacy with them which did not come so unself-consciously to adults more fixed in their ideas. As she was growing up bilingual, it is easy to imagine her skipping among the tepees, or watching the ceremonies, or joining in the singing, and, like the other girls, playing mother with wooden dolls in miniature cradleboards. Perhaps she participated in foot-races in the summer and top-spinning on the ice in winter and certainly she would have climbed into her father's wagon or ridden with him by horseback to visit their Indian or white neighbors, both those settled nearby and those, like her mother's family, across the Columbia River.

When Steele wrote to Meany in 1906 he also agreed to contribute something for Meany to print in his new publishing venture, the *Washington Magazine*. Whether he did so or not is impossible to ascertain, but nothing appeared;

later he certainly contemplated writing some articles about his old friend Chief Joseph and, interestingly, was adamant against using any Curtis portraits of the chief. As late as June 15, 1908, he wrote to Meany in this vein:

Dear Professor:—

I fully realize that you are a very busy man and feel rather timid to intrude on your valuable time. I have been contemplating on writing an article on Joseph for the Spokesman Review and would kindly ask you if you will give me a few details and data in regard to his birth, on causes leading up to his going on the warpath. I am acquainted with many of the facts but do not know but very little of his childhood and boyhood. I believe his wife stated that he was born at the Confluence of the In-ma-ha and another stream. I would like a brief history of his life but the main body of the article will be on my personal observation of all his characteristics during my 8 years of acquaintance and friendly intimacy with him. I will also defend his memory as to the vicious and virulent attacks of the Citizens of Idaho. I will give the details of his trip to Seattle and part of his speech at the University. The article will cover the humane and bright side of the noble Chieftain. I will also give a brief account of the unveiling here, the distinguished guests who were present, who spoke etc. I have a perfect photograph of Joseph taken in 1897, in the City of Washington. He is the real Joseph with full face a kindly expression and I feel assured no other is more perfect. If you will note the photograph taken by Curtis it is wretched and is not the real Joseph. I will use this photograph in my article. Now Professor, I shall feel grateful if you can furnish me with the desired information. I feel unable to conclude this brief letter without thanking you kindly for the "Quarterly" you are sending me also your beautiful song in music. I will be very much pleased if you will send me the measure of Mrs. Meany's feet, also the initial of her first name. With many pleasant remembrances and warm personal regards.

Very Truly
Henry M. Steele

Steele, as is so clear from his letters, deeply admired Joseph, probably did know him better than other white witnesses of the later years, and felt at home with Joseph's people. But, if he started to write, he did not finish. On October 2 of the year that he had written of his ambitions as an author in June, Dr. Latham sent Meany his version of what happened:

Dear Sir: Your letter arrived last night. Yes it is true that Henry M. Steele committed suicide on July 7th it was the most horrible tradgedy I have ever known.
Steele had become a perfect wreck from whisky and it was common talk here that Steele is getting nutty.

He had a little girl, Irene, she was a very beautiful child and very smart and bright, and of course was a great pet with us all, he seemed to worship that child and could not bear to have it out of his sight one minute. The act took place while they were eating supper. the little one was asleep in a side room and Mrs. Steele was writing on the table. he stepped into the room and slashed its throat with a razor almost severing its head from its body then immediately cut his own neck severing both the Jugular vein and corrotid artery, one of the men at the table ran for me but they were both dead before I got to the house.

The little one was raised here amongst the Indians. They all liked her and she knew them all and would speak their names very distinctly and rattle of those long twisted names that neither you nor I could repeat. it was in the midst of the July spree, but instantly all Horse Racing—Gambling and every thing stopped for two days until they were removed. It was simply terrible.

Dr. Latham's notion that the tragedy could be ascribed to alcoholism on Steele's part cannot be dismissed out of hand, but, like his view that Chief Joseph died of a broken heart, it should be thought of as a semi-hostile witness' half-truth; certainly, none of the other accounts of the incident mentioned Steele's drinking problem. And it is definite that Latham himself had difficulties with drink; on January 23, 1905 he wrote to his agent, Captain Webster: "I have reformed and am strictly on the Water Wagon. I am giving these fellows all good advise and offering myself as the terrible example."[46] A newspaper report of the double killing in the Spokane *Spokesman Review* of Friday, July 10, 1908, relied mainly on the ideas of George Steele, Henry's businessman brother. George Steele believed that Henry's final destructive acts took place during a bout of insanity that was related, in some way or other, to his intense love of Irene, his little daughter; the account therefore carried the title "Tragedy Traced to Love of Child." On the other hand, in the same newspaper item, Hal J. Cole, former agent for the Colville Reservation and probably responsible for Steele's initial employment at Nespelem, was insistent that Steele must have rationally contemplated suicide. During the period of political conventions, Steele had communicated with Cole about his intentions *vis à vis* "scratching his ticket," that is, voting: "I believe in what Roosevelt said," Steele had written, "a man who never scratches his ticket is not a good citizen. However, I do not expect to be here when the ballots are cast." Since the deaths took place in the July preceding the November elections—in fact, during the ceremonies over which Chief Joseph had presided for so many years—Steele was certainly not available to participate further in the political process.[47]

Joseph said, "We were contented to let things remain as the Great Spirit made them. [The white men] were not, and would change the rivers if they did not suit them." When the massive Chief Joseph Dam was being constructed on the Columbia at the edge of the Colville Reservation, some whites felt that a part of Joseph even more intimate than his name should be associated with it. The Bridgeport American Legion Post No. 218 formally resolved, with the support of the Seattle *Post-Intelligencer*, "that the body of the Nez Perce Chieftain, Chief Joseph, Hin-mah-too-yah-lat-kekt, Thunder-in-the-Mountains, be placed in the concrete of the Chief Joseph Dam."[48] As it happened, the authorities concerned were satisfied to place a bronze medal of Joseph on the wall of the powerhouse and a wreath at his grave in Nespelem prior to the formal dedication ceremonies at the dam itself in June 1956.

The bodies of the two Josephs have not been allowed to rest peacefully in their portions of earth. It was not until 1926 that Old Joseph's remains reached their final resting place when they were reburied, under a modest monument, at the foot of Lake Wallowa. Samuel Hill was astute, as might be expected, on the subject of property rights, and also, though he could not have known it, prophetic in this case: "By the way Meany," he wrote in April 1905, "don't you think we ought to get deeds running to the Historical Soc. for the little pieces of ground where we put these monuments up so that the descendants can't after a while come along and order us off?" No one was ever concerned to "order off" Joseph's monument, but as late as March 22, 1977 an Associated Press wire story—titled "Chief Joseph's Grave: A Matter of Honor" in the *Lewiston Morning News*—intimated that some Indians felt the remains should be better preserved, and possibly elsewhere.

Lucullus V. McWhorter, author of *Yellow Wolf* (1940) and intrepid collector of field material for what was to become a kind of oral history of the Nez Perces, *Hear Me, My Chiefs!* (1952), made a note on August 4, 1930:

By Chief Peo-peo Tholikt:—*"Chief Joseph, while living, talked that when he died he wished his body to be taken back to his own country, the Wallowa, and buried by the side of his father. He did not want his bones left in a strange land. There are now not many of his old band left, not many remaining of his warriors and fighters. It is left to you to see that this is done. Put it in the history that we are giving you; in the book we are making. If there is erected a statue to Chief Joseph, let it be in the Wallowa. There, he was raised, and there are the memories of his ancestors, their remains. Put it in the book we are making.*

The foregoing was delivered by Peo on the verge of breaking camp on the Clearwater, Aug. 4, 1930 after touring the major Idaho battle fields of the Nez Perce imbroglio, 1877. The subject had not been broached, and its introduction was wholly of his own volition. Yellow Wolf was asked for his opinion, and spoke briefly [in agreement].[49]

The following day, August 5, McWhorter recorded the same sentiment. This was only one of many times when the issue of moving Joseph's body was raised, and on other occasions, too, Peo-peo Tholekt, Yellow Wolf, and McWhorter were involved. During another effort, in 1920, Amos Wilkinson wrote to Meany with both vehemence and irony:

I received your letter 4th day of Jan 1920 stating if the people of Lewiston and Friends of Chief Joseph would raise about $10,000 or $15,000 to put up a fine big bronze statue of Chief Joseph in Lewiston so all could see him as he was in life. In my judgement the people of Lewiston and Friends of Chief Joseph can not raise this amount of money for statue etc. Do not think the body and monument will move better stay there for ever don't you think so Prof?

"Better stay there for ever don't you think so Prof?" These words must have echoed and re-echoed through Meany's mind, that summer of 1920. There were many tensions inherent in the matter. On September 12 McWhorter urged Meany to meet with Chief David Williams, Yellow Wolf, and Peo-peo Tholekt later in the month to discuss the possible removal and the erection of a new, materially superior, monument to both Chief Joseph and to his father, Old Joseph, concluding, "outraged while living, this last tribute of respect is due them from their dispoilers."[50]

After some delay due to the death of his mother, Meany replied to McWhorter that while he knew Joseph had always wanted to go back to the Wallowa, he "would not undertake to move those bones as long as his people at Nespelem want them left where they are. Those people must consent first. . . ."[51] He was undoubtedly wise to hold to this neutral position. He had already received a letter written on July 25, 1920 from the man who had interpreted between the Nez Perces and the Nespelems at the reburial ceremonies so many years earlier, David Williams. The letter ended:

We do not want Chief Joseph's body moved. . . . So do not pay any attention to Chief Peo-peo-n-talkl any more. We never told him to move Joseph's body. We don't want him to be moved.
  This is all.

I am
   Yours truly,
   David Williams
   Chief of the Nez Perce tribe

A few months later, on November 2, 1920, David Williams also died.

The earth and myself are of one mind. The measure of the land and the measure of our bodies are the same. . . . Do not misunderstand me, but understand me fully with reference to my affection for the land. I never said the land was mine to do with as I chose. The one who has the right to dispose of it is the one who has created it. . . .

Kopet. That is all.

ABBREVIATIONS

The following abbreviations are used in the notes and captions:

1. *Repositories*

AVERY — Frank F. Avery Photography Collection, Manuscripts Archives and Special Collections Division, Washington State University Library, Pullman

COLVILLE — Colville Indian Agency Records, Federal Archives and Records Center, Seattle, Washington

EXETER — University of Exeter Library, Exeter, England

HILL — Samuel Hill Papers, Maryhill Museum, Goldendale, Washington

LINDSLEY — Lawrence D. Lindsley Photography Collection, Photography Collection, Suzzallo Library, University of Washington, Seattle

MCWHORTER — L. V. McWhorter Collection, Manuscripts Archives and Special Collections Division, Washington State University Library, Pullman

MEANY — Edmond S. Meany Collection, University Archives and Records Center, University of Washington, Seattle. (Most of the documents reproduced in the text are from this collection, which is quite well indexed and arranged in chronological order; consequently, citations will be offered in the notes only for items less easy to trace or which are reproduced without a given date of writing or despatch.)

MIRES — Austin Mires Papers, Manuscripts Archives and Special Collections Division, Washington State University Library, Pullman

MHS — Montana Historical Society, Helena

MOORHOUSE — Lee Moorhouse Photography Collection, Oregon Collection, University of Oregon Library, Eugene

NAA — National Anthropological Archives, Washington, D.C.

NORTHWEST — Northwest Collection, Suzzallo Library, University of Washington, Seattle

OHS — Oregon Historical Society, Portland

UW — Photography Collection, Suzzallo Library, University of Washington, Seattle

WEBSTER — Papers of John McA. Webster, Manuscripts Archives and Special Collections Division, Washington State University Library, Pullman

2. *Publications*

Annual Report — *Annual Report of the Commissioner of Indian Affairs* (Washington, D.C.)

NAI — *The North American Indian* by Edward S. Curtis. Edited by Frederick Webb Hodge; fieldwork conducted under the patronage of J. Pierpont Morgan. Vol. 8 and Portfolio 8 (Norwood, Mass., 1911)

P-I — *Seattle Post-Intelligencer*

Times — *Seattle Times*

NOTES

Introduction

1. "Synopsis of Qualifications and Duties of Agency Physicians," *Annual Report*, 1889, pp. 492–94.

2. "Efficiency Reports, 1909," report by John McA. Webster (November 1909), Box 79, COLVILLE.

3. "Miscellaneous Matters: Farmers," *Annual Report*, 1889, pp. 11–12.

4. Albert M. Anderson to Austin Mires, June 25, 1900, MIRES.

5. Quoted in full in James Mooney, *The Ghost Dance Religion*, Bureau of American Ethnology, 14th Annual Report, Washington, D.C., 1896; reprinted in T. C. McLuhan, ed., *Touch the Earth* (New York: Outerbridge and Lazard, 1971; London: Abacus, 1973), p. 56.

6. *Annual Report*, 1898, p. 298.

7. *Annual Report*, 1900, p. 394.

Chronology

1. *NAI*, vol. 8, p. 161.

2. *NAI*, vol. 8, pp. 62–64; reprinted in M. Gidley, ed., *The Vanishing Race: Selections from Edward S. Curtis' "The North American Indian"* (London: David and Charles, 1976; New York: Taplinger, 1977), pp. 68–70.

3. Quoted by A. J. Cain in *Annual Report*, 1858, p. 277; reprinted in Alvin M. Josephy, *The Nez Perce Indians and the Opening of the Northwest*, abridged edition (New Haven and London: Yale University Press, 1971), p. 379.

4. *NAI*, vol. 8, p. 62.

5. Quoted in report from Monteith of February 9, 1877, published in *Annual Report of the Secretary of War* (Washington, D.C., 1877), vol. 1, p. 115.

6. Quoted in Seth K. Humphrey, *The Indian Dispossessed* (Boston: Houghton, Mifflin, 1905), p. 105.

7. Taken from the earliest known version as reproduced in Josephy 1971:609.

8. *North American Review* 128 (April 1879):412–33.

9. Quoted in Eugene B. Chase, "A Grand Aboriginal Function," *Northwest Magazine* 17, 8 (August 1899):20–21.

10. Holograph in Steele's hand in Chief Joseph file, Box 61, MEANY. Like the speech cited in note 11, this speech was originally enclosed in a letter from Steele to Meany, January 10, 1904.

11. Holograph in Steele's hand in Chief Joseph file, Box 61, MEANY.

12. Report in *The Red Man and Helper* (Carlisle, Pa.), March 18, 1904, p. 1; also in Helen A. Howard and Dan L. McGrath, *War Chief Joseph* (1941; reprint, Lincoln: University of Nebraska Press, 1964), p. 365.

13. Extract, slightly altered, from holograph in file labeled "Indians-Idaho-Chief Joseph," Box 61, MEANY.

Narrative

1. Farrand to Meany, November 28, 1905, MEANY.

2. Roosevelt to Meany, July 18, 1901, MEANY.

3. Cody to Meany, July 24, 1901, MEANY.

4. Chief Joseph file, Box 61, MEANY.

5. Edmond S. Meany, "Chief Joseph, the Nez Perce," Master's thesis, University of Wisconsin, 1901. Holograph version in Records Center, UW. The chapter is also reproduced in Howard and McGrath 1964:307–10.

6. McLaughlin to Secretary of the Interior, June 23, 1900 and July 3, 1900, Box 18, MEANY. These reports were forwarded to Meany by Commissioner Wesley A. Jones, with other documents, on July 29, 1901, Box 18, MEANY.

7. *Annual Report*, 1899, pp. 354–55.

8. La Roche to Meany, November 19, 1903, MEANY.

9. Latham to Meany, July 31, 1901, MEANY.

10. "Joseph Continues His Fight," *Times*, November 20, 1903, p. 8.

11. *P-I*, November 21, 1903, pp. 1, 11.

12. *P-I*, November 22, 1903. Clipping in Clarence Bagley scrapbook, no. 6, p. 64, NORTHWEST.

13. Holograph with note at the bottom, "Chief Joseph's Seattle address," in Chief Joseph file, Box 61, MEANY.

14. Latham to Acting Agent J. W. Bubb, March 10, 1894, Box 22, COLVILLE.

15. Steele to Meany, December 7, 1903, MEANY.

16. Steele to Meany, December 5, 1902, MEANY.

17. *Times*, October 2, 1904, p. 8.

18. *Annual Report*, 1904, pp. 122–23.

19. Newspaper clipping (Sept. 27, 1904) in Clarence Bagley scrapbook, no. 6, p. 65, NORTHWEST.

20. Latham to Acting Agent J. W. Bubb, March 1, 1894, Box 22, COLVILLE.

21. Latham to Bubb, June 30, 1895, Box 23, COLVILLE.

22. Meany to Samuel Hill, September 9, 1904, HILL. Quotation supplied by Ellen Welsh.

23. Meany to New England Granite and Marble Company, Seattle, May 27, 1905, Box 21, MEANY.

24. Meany to Steele, May 27, 1905. Letterpress book, University of Washington, State Historical Society Vol., MEANY.

25. Steele to Meany, May 28, 1905, MEANY.

26. Meany to Steele, June 11, 1905. Letterpress book, University of Washington State Historical Society Vol., MEANY.

27. Webster to Meany, June 16, 1905, MEANY.

28. Webster to Albert Waters, May 23, 1905, WEBSTER.

29. Latham to Meany, June 11, 1905, MEANY.

30. *P-I*, June 20, 1905, p. 1.

31. *P-I*, June 23, 1905, p. 3.

32. "Six Weeks among the Indians," newspaper clipping, August (?), 1905, in Clarence Bagley scrapbook, no. 5, p. 110, NORTHWEST.

33. Edward S. Curtis, "Vanishing Indian Types: The Tribes of the Northwest Plains," *Scribners Magazine* 39 (1906):657–71.

34. *NAI*, vol. 8, pp. 39–40.

35. Curtis to Harriet Leitch, September 22, 1950, E. S. Curtis folder, History Section, Seattle Public Library.

36. W. W. Phillips, "Beside an Old Chief's Resting Plot," unpublished paper in a private collection.

37. Meany to Samuel Hill, June 26, 1905, HILL. Quotation supplied by Ellen Welsh.

38. Edmond S. Meany, "Western Miniatures," unpublished typescript in Box 58, MEANY; photocopy in NORTHWEST.

39. Webster to Albert Waters, June 30, 1905, WEBSTER.

40. Steele to Meany, February 4, 1906, MEANY.

41. Meany to F. E. Leupp, January 5, 1906. Letterpress book, vol. 5, MEANY.

42. Webster to N. C. Titus, June 24, 1905, WEBSTER.

43. Meany to C. T. Brady, October 5, 1907. Letterpress book, vol. 6, MEANY.

44. Chief Joseph file, NORTHWEST, presumably transferred from MEANY at some time in the past.

45. Steele to Meany, July 26, 1906, MEANY.

46. Latham to Webster, January 23, 1905, WEBSTER.

47. "Tragedy Traced to Love of Child," *Spokesman-Review*, July 10, 1908, p. 7.

48. "Chief Joseph May Rest in Dam," *P-I*, June 15, 1950. Clipping in Chief Joseph file, NORTHWEST.

49. Statement recorded by L. V. McWhorter, August 4, 1930, MCWHORTER.

50. L. V. McWhorter to Meany, September 12, 1920, MCWHORTER.

51. Meany to L. V. McWhorter, September 27, 1920, MCWHORTER.

SOURCES OF ILLUSTRATIONS

1. Sepia print, Indians, UW
2. Glass negative, AVERY
3. Photogravure, private collection. Muhr's article was "A Gum-Biochromate Process for Obtaining Colored Prints from a Single Negative," *Camera Craft* 13 (August 1906):276–81.
4. Glass negative, AVERY
5. Print, Meany Bequest, UW
6. Print, Localities, UW
7. Print, Meany Bequest, UW
8. Glass negative, AVERY
9. Glass negative, LINDSLEY
10. Print, formerly attributed to T. W. Tolman, MHS
11. Glass negative, LINDSLEY
12. Print, Localities, UW
13. Glass negative, MOORHOUSE
14. Print, Indians, UW
15. Print, formerly attributed to T. W. Tolman, MHS
16. Glass negative, MOORHOUSE
17. Photogravure, originally titled "Nez Perce Brave," *NAI*, pl. 263, EXETER
18. Photogravure, originally titled "Nez Perce Babe," *NAI*, pl. 266, EXETER
19. Photogravure, originally titled "Holiday Trappings—Cayuse," *NAI*, pl. 273, EXETER
20. Photogravure, *NAI*, facing p. 42, EXETER
21. Photogravure, *NAI*, pl. 261, EXETER
22. Photogravure, *NAI*, facing p. 6, EXETER
23. Print, NAA
24. Print, Indians, UW
25. Photogravure, *NAI*, facing p. 24, EXETER
26. Print, Indians, UW
27. Glass negative, LINDSLEY
28. Sepia print, Indians, UW
29. Glass negative, LINDSLEY
30. Chief Joseph file, Box 61, MEANY
31. Print, Meany Bequest, UW
32. Print, Thomas Prosch Album No. 1, UW (identified as a Latham photograph by Prosch)
33. Glass negative, LINDSLEY
34. Print, Meany Bequest, UW
35. Print, Meany Bequest, UW
36. Print, Indians (marked Meany Bequest), UW
37. Print, Localities (marked Meany Bequest), UW

38. Print, Meany Bequest, UW
39. Print, Thomas Prosch Album No. 1, UW, with comment by Prosch. (The newspaper item was Vella Winner, "Choosing Chief Joseph's Successor," *Oregon Sunday Journal* (Portland), December 25, 1904; clipping in MCWHORTER.)
40. Photogravure, NAI, pl. 256, EXETER
41. Photogravure, originally titled "Typical Nez Perce," *NAI*, pl. 258, EXETER
42. Photogravure, NAI, facing p. 20, EXETER
43. Postcard, Indians (postals), UW
44. Glass negative, LINDSLEY
45. Print, Indians (marked Meany Bequest), UW. (There is also a print in Thomas Prosch Album No. 1, UW. The summary of Chica-ma-poo's life was found in Box 58, MEANY.)
46. Print, Indians, UW
47. Print, Indians, UW
48. Print, Indians, UW
49. Print, MHS
50. Photogravure, *NAI*, facing p. 38, EXETER
51. Print in Edmond S. Meany Album No. 4, UW
52. Glass negative, MOORHOUSE
53. Glass negative, MOORHOUSE
54. Sepia print, Curtis, UW
55. Sepia print, Curtis, UW
56. Glass negative, MOORHOUSE
57. Sepia print, Curtis, UW
58. Sepia print, Curtis, UW
59. Photogravure, *NAI*, facing p. 40, EXETER
60. Print, LINDSLEY
61. Photogravure, originally titled "A War Chief—Nez Perce," *NAI*, pl. 271, EXETER
62. Print in an album of Latham's Indian pictures owned by the Rainier Club, Seattle
63. Glass negative, LINDSLEY
64. Photogravure, NAI, pl. 265, EXETER
65. Print, Meany Bequest, UW. (Enclosed with letter from Fred R. Meyer to Meany, October 20, 1907, MEANY).
66. Photogravure, NAI, facing p. 26, EXETER
67. Print, Meany Bequest, UW
68. Print, NAA
69. Print, OHS
70. Photogravure, originally titled "Nez Perce Warrior," *NAI*, pl. 262, EXETER. (Identified by comparison with many other pictures of Peo-peo by Latham and others.)
71. Print, Indians (marked Meany Bequest), UW
72. Print, MEANY

FURTHER READING AND RESEARCH:
A BIBLIOGRAPHIC ESSAY

Unpublished materials

I hope it will be apparent from the contents of this book that the manuscript sources on which it is based have not been as fully exploited as they might have been. It is true that some doctoral dissertations have derived from the Colville Agency Records, but a mere glance at Daniel Rooney's *Bibliographical Essay* on the collections (available at the Federal Archives and Records Center) demonstrates that it would be possible— if an insane endeavor—to reconstruct a day-to-day life of the agency for almost any given period.

The neglect by historians of the Meany Papers, the principal source of the documents here, is even more surprising, though the later boxes (such as numbers 58 and 61), which are stuffed with documents of all kinds, have not been thoroughly indexed. Similarly, Samuel Hill had his fingers in so many big pies that his papers would repay thorough investigation. It was fortunate for me that the Avery and Lindsley collections of photographic images came into good archivists' hands at just the time I was seeking such pictures; it may be that more has been discovered about Avery while I have been working on this book in England. In the same way, lack of easy access prevented me from extracting more from the Moorhouse Collection; that there is more is virtually certain, since Moorhouse visited Nespelem once before his journey to the reburial and made a photographic record of it. It is for reasons such as these that I confess in the Introduction that the present book was derived by "opportunism out of serendipity."

Published materials

In the case of published materials, a rather bold map of the terrain has already been laid down by previous writers.

Nez Perce History and Ethnography

The one indispensable work on Nez Perce history based on original research is Alvin M. Josephy's *The Nez Perce Indians and the Opening of the Northwest* (New Haven and London: Yale University Press, 1965). Besides all that is promised by its title, the book includes reproductions of some of Latham's photographs, though they are attributed to T. W. Tolman. It also includes an epilogue specifically devoted to Chief Joseph, but it says very little on his later years. The version of Josephy's book cited in the present work is the abridged edition of 1971. A rather disorganized but fascinating work is L. V. McWhorter's "oral history" of the Nez Perces, *Hear Me, My Chiefs* (Caldwell, Idaho: Caxton Press, 1952). There are numerous other works of a general nature and some of these will be mentioned below; of these, those by Merrill D. Beal and Helen Addison Howard are probably the most helpful.

It will be obvious that because the point of view for much of the present book is that of a group of "white witnesses" to Joseph's end, and because these men showed relatively little interest in ethnography—indeed, one of them, Barnett Stillwell, actually wrote to Professor Meany that he had spent all his spare time on the reservation prospecting for gold rather than pursuing what he called "folklore stories"—there is little here of ethnographic significance. Nevertheless, one of the witnesses was responsible for a most important ethnographic treatise, and I did rely on it: the eighth volume of Edward S. Curtis' *The North American Indian* (Norwood, Mass., 1911). Other useful ethnographic studies are Herbert J. Spinden, *The Nez Perce Indians*, Memoirs of the American Anthropological Society (Lancaster, Penn., 1908) and Verne F. Ray, *Ethnohistory of the Joseph Band of Nez Perce Indians, 1805–1905*, Indian Claims Commission Docket No. 186 (New York: Garland, 1974).

A good book on the history and sociology of reservations in general is sorely needed, and there certainly is not one that deals at all fully with the particular experience of the Colville Nez Perces. Insight into white policies (and ideas) concerning Indians in this era is provided by Francis P. Prucha's collection, *Americanizing the American Indians: Writings by the "Friends of the Indian," 1880–1900* (Cambridge, Mass.: Harvard University Press, 1973). Much information about life on the Colville Reservation (not just for Moses' Columbias but also for other tribes) can be found in the later chapters of Robert H. Ruby and John A. Brown, *Half-Sun on the Columbia: A Biography of Chief Moses* (Norman, Okla.: University of Oklahoma Press, 1965). My own *With One Sky Above Us: Life on an Indian Reservation at the Turn of the Century* (New York: Putnam, 1979; London: Windward/Webb & Bower, 1979) constitutes a briefer examination. A work that examines some aspects of more recent Nez Perce experience is Deward E. Walker, *Conflict and Schism in Nez Perce Acculturation: A Study of Religion and Politics* (Pullman, Wash.: Washington State University Press, 1968).

Chief Joseph

Chief Joseph's own life story has been told a number of times, most reliably by Helen Addison Howard and Dan L. McGrath in a book first published in 1941, *War Chief Joseph* (Lincoln, Neb.: University of Nebraska Press, 1964). As the title suggests, however, this book overemphasizes Joseph's military role at the expense of his spiritual position. Alvin M. Josephy's *The Patriot Chiefs* (New York: Viking, 1961) is mostly edifying because Joseph's portrait is ranged alongside that of other major Indian leaders. On specific events in Joseph's life the following, together with works already mentioned, were found reliable or interesting. On the Nez Perce War of 1877: Merrill D. Beal, *I Will Fight No More Forever* (Seattle and London: University of Washington Press, 1963) and L. V. McWhorter, *Yellow Wolf: His Own Story* (London: Abacus, 1977), a classic first published in 1940. On the situation leading up to and in 1879, Joseph's own account is certainly the most readable: "An Indian's View of Indian Affairs," *North American Review* 128 (April 1879):412–33. One of the early books by a white person who took up his cause was Helen Hunt Jackson's *Century of Dishonor* (New York, 1881; reprinted in various editions). There is a brief treatment of the chief's visits to the Wallowa Valley in 1899 and 1900 in Caroline Wasson Thomason, "Chief Joseph's Return to His Beloved Wallowa," *Spokesman-Review*, magazine (August 16, 1953), p. 2; McLaughlin's less friendly version of the second of these visits was printed in *My Friend the Indian* (Boston, 1910), pp. 344–46. It is likely that further light would be shed on Joseph's relationship with the Indian inspector through an examination of the relevant files in McLaughlin's papers, and they would certainly have much to say about the events leading up to the opening of the north half of the Colville Reservation under the terms of the McLaughlin Agreement; the papers are housed at Assumption Abbey, Richardton, North Dakota, under the care of Father Pfaller.

Joseph's 1903 visit to Washington, D.C. and New York—and, indeed, some other events and sayings of his last years—were reported by one of Meany's correspondents, Cyrus T. Brady, in *Northwestern Fights and Fighters* (New York, 1907; reprinted by University of Nebraska Press, 1979). Among the historians who mistakenly believed that the chief visited Seattle in 1903 at the invitation of James J. Hill were Merrill D. Beal *(I Will Fight No More Forever)* and Chester A. Fee *(Chief Joseph: The Biography of a Great Indian* [New York: Wilson-Erickson, 1936]). Newspaper accounts of the visit, which supplement those quoted in the text of the present work, include "Joseph Tells His Story," *Seattle Times* (November 21, 1903), p. 7; "Chief Joseph Comes to Town," *Seattle Star* (November 21, 1903), p. 5; and the story in the University of Washington student magazine *Pacific Wave* 11, 10 (November 25, 1903):4.

Joseph's death was, of course, widely reported at the time; among the historians who later recorded that it was caused predominantly or exclusively by "a broken heart" were Merrill Beal (p. 300), Alvin Josephy (p. 643), Doris Shannon Garst in *Chief Joseph of the Nez Perces* (New York: Julian Messner, 1953), p. 177, and Mark A. Brown, *The Flight of the Nez Perce* (New York: Putnam, 1967), p. 431. By contrast, the reburial ceremonies were, it seems, only reported in those newspapers to which Professor Meany or Lee Moorhouse had access, and most such accounts are at least mentioned elsewhere in this book; the only historian to offer a brief description was Chester Fee in his biography of Chief Joseph, pp. 303–4.

Although many of the works cited above reflect or contribute to the myth of Joseph, none examines it. What is needed now, I think, is a study something like Philip Young's probing treatment of the myth of Pocahontas in his essay "The Mother of Us All," *Kenyon Review* 24 (Summer 1962):391–415 (reprinted several times). Just as Young takes his evidence from histories, poems, pictures, and drama, such an essay devoted to Joseph would need to pay attention to the photographs and other visual representations—his iconography, so to speak. Terry Abraham of Washington State University Library is diligently documenting such pictorial representations; this will provide the raw material for such an approach.

The Witnesses

It is obvious that all the people whose views of Joseph are recorded in this book looked through (or struggled to remove) culturally tinted spectacles. Some analysis of white ideas of Native Americans is to be found in various chapters of Thomas F. Gossett, *Race: The History of an Idea in America* (New York: Schocken, 1965) and, very fully, in Roy Harvey Pearce's major work, *Savagism and Civilization* (Baltimore: Johns Hopkins University Press, 1953; reprinted 1965).

A fairly recent study which develops some of Pearce's insights into the loose racial ideology—"savagism"—that influenced all these men (and with a more general application than its title would suggest) is the first chapter of Robert F. Sayre's *Thoreau and the American Indians* (Princeton: Princeton University Press, 1977). On a more prosaic level, an excellent comprehensive bibliography is Francis P. Prucha's *A Bibliographical Guide to the History of Indian-White Relations in the United States* (Chicago and London: University of Chicago Press, 1977). Specific sources of information on each of my chosen witnesses are recorded below.

ALBERT M. ANDERSON. Much of the basic data on Anderson—as on most of the others—comes from a perusal of the relevant directories and gazetteers for Spokane and the various counties of the "Big Bend" region, from an examination of the U.S. Census for 1900 (for which both Latham and Steele served as enumerators), and from the various lists of Bureau employees in the Colville Agency Records (Box 152), and in the published *Annual Reports*. In addition, the Spokane newspapers were useful to me, especially as they were so well indexed by a team of Works Progress Administration workers in the thirties; using these indexes in Spokane Public Library it was possible to find obituaries for and news stories concerning Anderson and some of the others. Anderson's obituary on page 6 of the *Spokesman-Review* of August 21, 1928 was titled "Major Anderson Saw Wild West" and, interestingly enough, it carried the subtitle, "Chief Joseph's Keeper." A sketch of "the Major" also appeared in Richard Steele *et al.*, *An Illustrated History of the Big Bend Country* (Spokane, 1904), pp. 471–72. A more interior view of the man was achieved, of course, by reading a good portion of his own correspondence as agent and all his letters to Professor Meany. Much could be done to unravel the exact nature of his culpability for corrupt financial practices during his term as agent, and, possibly, as a right-of-way agent for the railroads. A start was made by Delbert Clear in his Master's thesis on Capt. John McA. Webster (Washington State University, 1962), but there are numerous relevant papers still awaiting examination in the Colville Agency Records; Box 71, for example, is stuffed with such documents. Two letters by Webster now in his own papers present his view very fully, one to the Commissioner of Indian Affairs of February 6, 1905, and one to Thomas R. Benton, attorney for the Great Northern Railway, of November 15, 1905.

EDWARD S. CURTIS. For Curtis much more information is currently in the public domain. The most reliable accounts of his life and work appear in Ralph W. Andrew's pioneering book *Curtis' Western Indians* (Seattle and New York: Superior, 1962), though this contains no documentation; T. C. McLuhan's Introduction to *Portraits from North American Indian Life* (New York: Outerbridge and Lazard, 1972; London: Barrie and Jenkins, 1973); two similar books by Florence Curtis Graybill and Victor Boesen, *Edward S. Curtis: Visions of a Vanishing Race* (New York: Crowell, 1976) and *Edward S. Curtis: Photographer of the North American Indian* (New York: Dodd, Mead, 1977); and Bill Holm and George Quimby, *Edward S. Curtis in the Land of the War Canoes* (Seattle and London: University of Washington Press, 1980). The information in these books was supplemented and occasionally corrected by my own research into many hundreds of unpublished materials by and about Curtis; a fraction of the results of this work may be seen in my "Edward S. Curtis Speaks . . . ," *History of Photography* 2 (October 1978):347–54. It was also most gratifying to be granted access to the unpublished memoir (quoted in the text) written by Curtis' first really important assistant, William W. Phillips. Phillips saw the initial volumes of *The North American Indian* through the press.

EDWARD H. LATHAM. Raw data on Latham—such little as I was able to discover— was incorporated and cited in my book on him, *With One Sky Above Us* (mentioned earlier), and this includes a number of letters and a long report he wrote for publication on pages 492–94 of the *Annual Report* of 1892. As his images become better known, it may well be the case—and it is certainly to be hoped—that more photographs will be discovered and that other aspects of his life and work will be revealed.

EDMOND S. MEANY. Meany's life deserves the devotion of a biography and it is pleasing to report that Professor George Frykman of Washington State University is working on one. A brief authoritative sketch by Kent D. Richards appeared in *Arizona and the West* 17 (Autumn 1975):201–4. The notebook covering his 1901 visit to

Nespelem is in Box 70 of his papers, in a file marked "Personal papers of E. S. Meany." The Northwest Collection contains a very full bibliography of Meany's works compiled by Ronald Todd (1935), with various supplements; it was by using this that I was able to find many of the unsigned newspaper items that are quoted from or reproduced in this book. Relevant items of some substance consulted for this book, which are mentioned but not cited elsewhere, include "Highest Type of Indian," *Seattle Times*, June 13, 1905, p. 3, and "Yellow Bird Scouts," *Post-Intelligencer*, June 30, 1905, p. 9. Meany's friend Lee Moorhouse wrote an illustrated article, "The Umatilla Indian Reservation," *The Coast* 15, 4 (April 1908):235–50; and earlier, probably in 1905, he issued a *Souvenir Album of Noted Indian Photographs* (Pendleton, Oregon). For Meany's relationship with Frederick Jackson Turner, see Roy Lokken, "As One Historian to Another: Frederick Jackson Turner's Letters to Edmond S. Meany," *Pacific Northwest Quarterly* 44 (January 1953):30–39.

HENRY M. STEELE. On Steele there was, of course, very little published evidence for me to find. Many of his letters, however, appear in the Colville Agency Records under the heading "Letters sent by Agency Farmers." The most crucial letters to Anderson by Thomas McCrossen informing on Steele were written on October 29, November 4, and November 7, 1901, and appear on pages 119, 126, and 131 of Letterpress Book 1 in Box 331. Erskine Wood's memories of his time at Nespelem were published first in 1893 and most recently as a pamphlet titled *Days with Chief Joseph* by the Oregon Historical Society (Portland, 1972). Lora Begg's pamphlet, *Nespelem—Then and Now*, a copy of which is in the Manuscripts, Archives and Special Collections Division of Washington State University Library, was published in 1955. Also, like Latham, he is mentioned with some frequency in the Ruby and Brown study of Chief Moses.

BARNETT STILLWELL. There was an even more marked paucity of information on Stillwell, especially after he moved to Jerome, Idaho. He was always keen to apply for civil service jobs, however, and would write to Meany seeking his support and that of Professor A. H. Yoder, a former classmate at Madison State Normal, South Dakota; from such letters, especially that to Meany of September 20, 1924, it was just possible to sketch his career.

JOHN McA. WEBSTER. The prominence of Webster's official position has ensured that more data on him has survived. There is much information, including his 1909 Seattle speech, in the two boxes of his own papers (together with some fine photographs of him in the Avery collection), and voluminous materials in the Colville Agency Records. He has a chapter devoted to him in *The Spokane Indians: Children of the Sun* (Norman, Okla.: University of Oklahoma Press, 1970), by Robert Ruby and John A. Brown, and Delbert K. Clear wrote a good basic monograph on him in his Master's thesis for Washington State University, "Captain John McAdam Webster, Indian Agent 1904–1914: A Decade of Honorable Service" (1962). Meany's short piece, "Captain Webster Loves His Work," appeared on page 12 of the *Post-Intelligencer* of July 9, 1905, a page which also contains Meany items on Fort Spokane as an Indian school, Chief Skolaskin, and Joseph La Fleur, an old-time French-Canadian Indian trader; the page is illustrated by Frank Avery's photographs. One of Webster's correspondents, Nelson C. Titus, eventually wrote an essay on the Nez Perces, which was published in Meany's journal: "Last Stand of the Nez Perces," *Washington Historical Quarterly* 6 (Summer 1915):145–53.

It is also pleasant to record that the man who took over from Henry Steele as additional farmer at Nespelem, who spied on Steele, and who Webster asked to police the reburial ceremonies, Thomas McCrossen, eventually mellowed into a sympathetic friend to the Indians at Nespelem. In 1908 he helped James H. Teit gather ethnographic information for "The Middle Columbia Salish," which was edited by Franz Boas and published in *University of Washington Publications in Anthropology* 2, 4 (June 1928):83–128.

INDEX

Numbers in boldface refer to illustrations or their captions

Ollicott (Joseph's nephew), 73, 80, 83
Ollokot (Joseph's brother), 27, 29, 30, 47
Olympia, Washington, 5
Oregon, 4, 15, 24, 25, 26, 37, 56, 70
Oregon Sunday Journal, The, 83
Out West, 9, 68
Owhi (Nez Perce), 68

Pacific Monthly, 9
Pacific Northwest, The (Meany), 9
Page, Walter Hines, 87
Parsons, Mrs., 62
Pendleton, Oregon, 4, 75, **14**
Peo-peo Tholekt, 83, 91–92, **70**
Perry, Captain David, 28, 29
Peter, king of Servia, 69
Phillips, William W., 6, 78, 82, 87
Pio-pio Mox-mox. *See* Yellow Bird
Plateau culture, 13, 47
Plenty Coups, Chief, 55
Plymouth, Massachusetts, 78
Poker Joe, 29, 30
Ponca Reservation, Oklahoma, 34, 35
Portland, Oregon, 6, 35, 74, 83
Port Orchard, Washington, 6
Pratt, Colonel Enoch, **26**
Presbyterians, 24
Price, J. H., 5
Prince, George, **5**
Puckmiakin, 48
Puget Sound, 6, 80
Puget Sound, College of, 8
Puget Sound Magazine, 9
Pullman, Washington, 4

Quadra, Bodega y, 70
Quapaw Reservation, Kansas Territory, 31
Quilliute Reservation, Washington, 44

Rains, Lieutenant Sevier M., 28
Rawn, Captain Charles C., 29
Records Center, University of Washington, 3
Red Cloud, Chief, 55, **65**
Redington, John Watermelon, 87
Red Thunder (Joseph's nephew), 55, 56, 58, 60, 63, 71, **1, 43**
Reuben, Chief, 27
Reuben, James, 34, 35
Reuner, Ella, 6
Riis, Jacob, 61
Roosevelt, President Theodore, 6, 38, 43, 69, 90
Ruby, Robert H., 5
Russo-Japanese War (1904), 69

St. Louis Exposition (1904), 39, 75
Salish language group, 13, 15, **62**
Salmon River, 28

San Juan Island, Washington, 70
San Poil River, 13
San Poils (tribe), 13
Sawyer, Wells M., **68**
Scott, R. B., 54
Scribner, J. S., 61
Scribner's Magazine, 6, 76
Seattle, Washington: Curtis' photographic studio in, 6, 55; Joseph visits, 55–61; mentioned, 3, 4, 8, 9, 12, 17, 37, 43, 49, 52, 65, 78, 89, **3, 5, 18**
Seattle Daily Trade Journal, 9
Seattle Post-Intelligencer: Meany writes for, 8, 10, 54, 75, 78, 82, 84, 85; reports Joseph's visit to Seattle, 56–61; mentioned, **46,** 68, 91
Seattle Times, 10, 54, 56, 65, 74
Shaffer, Rosemary Alice. *See* Steele, 'Mary
Shahaptiarn language group, 13, **62**
Sidney. *See* Port Orchard, Washington
Sioux, 30, 48, 86, **45, 65**
Sitting Bull, Chief, 18, 30, 31, 35, 48
Skagit River, 3
Skolaskin, Chief, 13, 15
Smithsonian Institution, 7, 43
Smohalla, 15
Snake River, 23
South Carolina, 85
South Half. *See* Colville Reservation
Spalding, Eliza, 23
Spalding, Henry, 23, 24
Spining, Howard, 75
Spokane, Fort. *See* Fort Spokane
Spokane, Washington, 5, 6, 7, 51, 52, 54, 65, 73
Spokane Falls. *See* Spokane
Spokane Reservation, Washington, 6, 12, **2, 8**
Spokanes (tribe), 13, **8**
Spokesman Review, 75, 89, 90
Stanford University, 43
Steaves, Robert A., 11
Steele, George, 10, 90
Steele, Henry M.: biographical sketch of, 10–11; resigns from Indian service, 53–54; death of, 89–90; quoted, 20, 49–50, 65, 70–71, 72–74, 84, 89, **44, 72;** mentioned, 3–4, 5, 12, 17, 19, 44–48 *passim,* 55, 58, 60–64 *passim,* 74, 75, 82, 86, **6, 7, 37**
Steele, Irene, 4, 11, 84, 88, 90
Steele, 'Mary, 11, 84, 90
Steptoe, Lieutenant Colonel Edward J., 25
Steubenville, Ohio, 12
Stevens, Governor I. C., 25, 26
Steveson, E. T.: store of, 47, 51
Stillwell, Ada, 11, 50, 55, 88, **7, 38, 67**
Stillwell, Barnett: biographical sketch of, 11–